W9-CHL-902

Curious Boating Inventions

Curious Boating Inventions

Joachim Schult

Translated by **Inge Moore**

Taplinger Publishing Co., Inc. New York

First published in the United States in 1974
by TAPLINGER PUBLISHING CO., INC.
New York, New York

First published under the title *Aus der Jugendzeit
des Motorbootes* by Verlag Delius, Klasing & Co,
Bielefeld-Berlin, 1971
Published in Great Britain by Elek Books Limited, London

Library of Congress Catalog Card Number: 74–1525
ISBN 0–8008–2103–3

Printed in Great Britain.

Contents

INTRODUCTION

Inventions are like visiting cards of an era. Patents not only reflect the technological attitude of an age, they also reflect all the pipe-dreams and hopeful aspirations of its contemporaries. Among them we find man's greatest achievements and the inception of new ideas that have changed the world, like those of Daimler and Diesel.

There are also less spectacular inventions, which we now take for granted without realizing that they, too, were original and patented ideas like the celebrated achievements of more famous men. Yachtsmen should remind themselves of the kapok filling in lifejackets, which must have saved thousands of people from a watery death, or the transom of inflatable boats, without which there would be nowhere to hang the powerful outboard motors necessary for their sparkling performance.

Inventions are children of their time. They happen almost inevitably when the technological climate is right and people have a need for them. For this very reason they are such valuable historical documents, whether they remained mere ideas or were turned into mass production, whether they were put into practice immediately or not until much later. With mixed feelings of sadness and mirth, half amazed and half amused, we contemplate this collection of brainwaves of yesteryear, some of which never developed beyond technical fragments. The waterski, for example, which started off as a clumsy displacement device, until lightweight materials and powerful marine engines encouraged its development into what it is today and made water-skiing into a fast sport, which is enjoyed all over the world.

We realize that yachting as a popular sport had some of its roots in fairly unlikely inventions that we never knew about: paddle-driven swimming frames, water-velocipedes with paddle wheels, inflatable water wheels and a multitude of other devices which our forbears had to move along by muscular effort until light engines and materials favoured the development of fast outboard planing boats. Today's popular sport of motorboating with its speedboats, pocket cruisers and seaworthy family yachts has developed as much from curious inventions like these as it has from the large motor yachts of the wealthy.

To recognize and prove this parallel development is an interesting and worthwhile undertaking. People have always dreamed of travelling across the water in their own craft, but not until recently have ordinary people been able to enjoy this pastime at acceptable cost.

I have dedicated this book to my children. Born in the 'affluent fifties', educated in the 'golden sixties' and boat-owners in the 'fascinating seventies' they are more likely than the previous generation to lose sight of the long path of evolution and the multitude of individual creative efforts which are manifest in every aspect of our perfected world, even in the automatic light on a lifebuoy or the valve on a lifejacket. May they, and all my other readers, get to know and understand the people who before and for us laid the foundations to watersport as the popular leisure activity which we now enjoy. They could do no more than dream and invent; we can put their dreams into practice and enjoy them. It is only fair that we should pay tribute to them.

Joachim Schult
Hamburg, May 1971

1 Foot Propulsion and Paddlewheel Curiosities

Fig. 1 Swimming apparatus by Tricornot, France, 1899.

On 9 October 1886 Gottlieb Daimler registered the patent for an 'installation for driving a ship's screw by means of a gas or petrol/paraffin motor'. In the same year he installed his 1.5 hp motor in a boat, which he tested on the River Neckar and which reached a speed of 10 kmph.

In 1898 Sir Charles Parsons' *Turbinia,* fitted with a 2000 hp steam turbine reached a top speed of 35 knots and became the first vessel to escape the wave system of displacement hulls. If we consider these events as the beginnings of motorboating, then some of the ideas featured in this book could be said to belong to a period prior to motorboat history as we know it. They are, so-to-speak, pre-historic.

Granted, there are amusing and even ridiculous devices among them, which one can scarcely imagine on the water. But they are very much children of a time when there were no motor vehicles and the only power was from horses; when sailing ships and paddle steamers plied the seas and people travelled by Shanks's pony, or, if they wanted to be very sporting, on a velocipede.

It was in those days that people first discovered the water as something to bathe in. Gradually, bathing beaches became popular, where wooden beach huts for ladies and gentlemen were set up at respectable distances from one another. Bathing carts were wheeled into the sea and from their shelter the trendsetters of society, boldly clad in long bathing suits, slipped into the cooling waves. But how many of those desporting themselves in this fashion could swim?

Thus the desire to swim in and ride on the water encouraged the invention of numerous pieces of apparatus. A typical example is the swimming machine by the Frenchman Tricornot which was patented in 1899

9

(Fig. 1). The person using it lies between two longitudinal bearers which are fitted with sliding panels with hinged flaps. These the user operates with his hands or feet.

Similar to some of the subsequent devices this apparatus was intended to multiply the effect of muscular

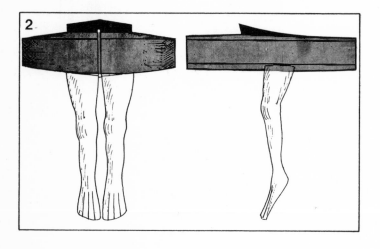

effort and 'protect the person from sinking if he should be overcome by fatigue'. How many hours anyone shackled to this rather inadequately buoyant device could survive is unknown.

One obvious invention, which would have been typical of this prehistoric period, was actually not made till 1951 by Johann Seidenberger of Kerschlach in Bavaria, Germany. It is a boat with foot propulsion! Attached to openings in the bottom of the hull are boots made of waterproof material (Fig. 2), into

which a person climbs from above. An important point is that: 'the portion of the boots enclosing the thigh and calf must be made of stronger material than that around the knee and foot. The foot part must be flexible in such a way that it bends aft as the leg is moved forward but offers resistance to the water as the leg is moved aft.'

But let us turn to historic patents. Around 1880 the German Imperial Patent Office had not yet decided on how to classify these novel water vehicles and registered them in turn under 'Sport', 'Saddlery and Coachbuilding', and 'Ship Building and Operation'.

The close relationship between the sports of sailing and motorboating is illustrated by the water velocipede invented by Carl Zenker of Breslau, Poland (Fig. 3) and patented in 1880. The paddlewheels on either side can be operated by the feet via a crank shaft, but this is also linked to a wind turbine by a rope belt. The idea is that the wind enters a funnel shaped rather like an old-fashioned gramophone horn, which directs it to two vertical wind wheels. The funnel can be turned into the prevailing wind direction via lines leading aft at either side.

The inventor says nothing about how the air thus captured is to escape again, nor has he obviously stopped to think that with a following wind there will be no air movement into the funnel, because the wind created by forward movement largely cancels out the following wind. On the other hand, if the wind is from

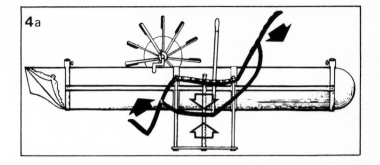

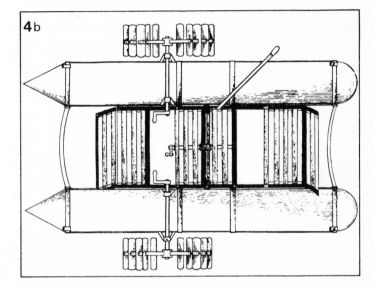

any other quarter, it would seem that the result is merely a stagnating air mass.

The 'bathing apparatus' designed by Joseph Estner of Munich, Germany, in 1881 was rather more promising. It consisted of two cylinders made of strong sheet metal arranged in a parallel position 2 ft apart. They were 6 ft 8 in long and 1 ft in diameter, and each was divided up into three watertight compartments. They were joined together by curved iron girders (Figs 4a

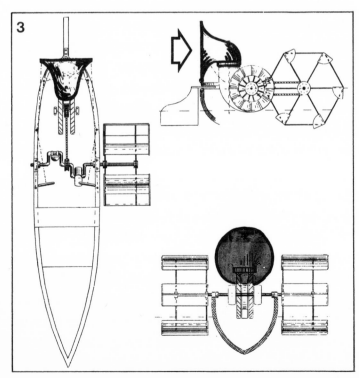

and 4b), and in the middle between them there was a chair with adjustable back rest. To move the vehicle, the person sitting in it operated two paddlewheels 28 inches in diameter via handles at either side. If he wished to bathe he did not even have to leave his chair but could simply lower it into the water on a toothed bar.

The 'Central-Velocipede for land and water travel' invented by Paul Ficker of Reutlingen, Germany, in 1881 (Figs 5a and 5b) does not offer such delightful versatility. The most its driver can hope for are wet feet. He sits in a suspended seat between the two large paddlewheels, which he turns with surprisingly small handles. Where this apparatus is to get its buoyancy

Figs. 5a and 5b 'Central-velocipede for travel on land and water' by Paul Ficker, Reutlingen, Germany, 1881.

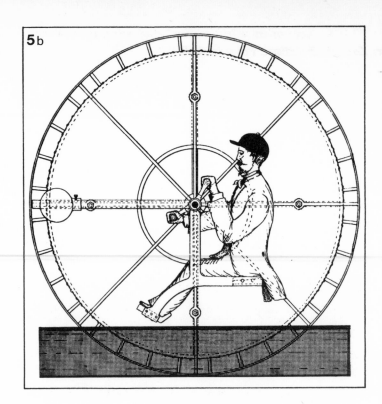

from the inventor does not say; apparently it was intended for shallow water only.

By comparison the 'Water-Velocipede' by Eugen Schreiner of Berlin, which was patented in 1884, is very soundly constructed (Fig. 6). Two narrow floats connected by girders support a wheel, which the driver, sitting in a saddle astride the wheel, turns by means of pedals (Fig. 7). The wheel itself does not propel the vehicle but drives a four-bladed propeller

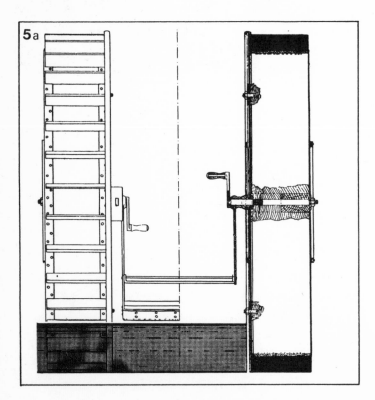

via a continuous rope that runs over a pulley wheel at the stern. The multihull idea and the type of propeller drive were far ahead of their time.

The same cannot be said of J. Friedrich of Breslau, Poland. In his tricycle large, air-tight balloons with a carrying capacity of 330 lbs take the place of wheels. When submerged in the water their under-water section becomes triangular. Propulsion comes from a paddlewheel with pedal drive, which is situated between the rear balloon wheels (Fig. 8).

To give his velocipede a rather more pleasing appearance, the inventor disguises it as a swan (Fig. 9): 'The neck of the swan serves as steering column. Steering is done by means of reins which are fastened to a stick carried in the swan's beak . . . The swan's wings are hinged and can be spread out so that, when the vehicle is used on the water, the wind's driving force can be utilized.' One wonders whether, perhaps, the inventor was employed as stage designer by the

*Fig. 6   'Water velocipede' by Eugen Schreiner, Berlin,
Germany, 1884 (side view).*

*Fig. 7   'Water velocipede' by Eugen Schreiner, Berlin,
1884 (sectional view).*

*Fig. 8   Paddlewheel velocipede by J. Friedrich, Breslau,
Poland, 1885.*

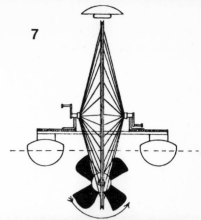

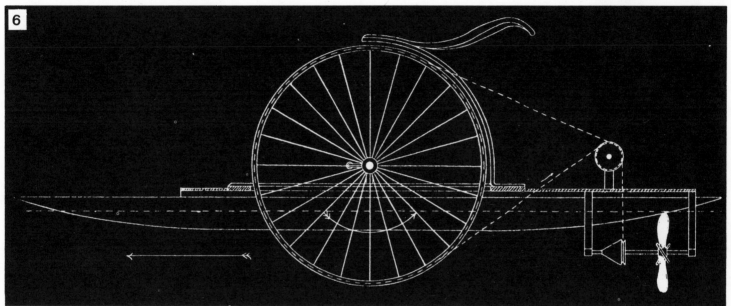

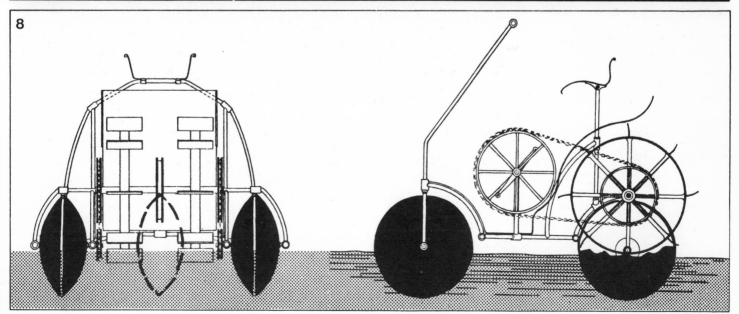

Fig. 9 Swan-disguise for water velocipede by J. Fried-rich, Breslau, Poland, 1885.

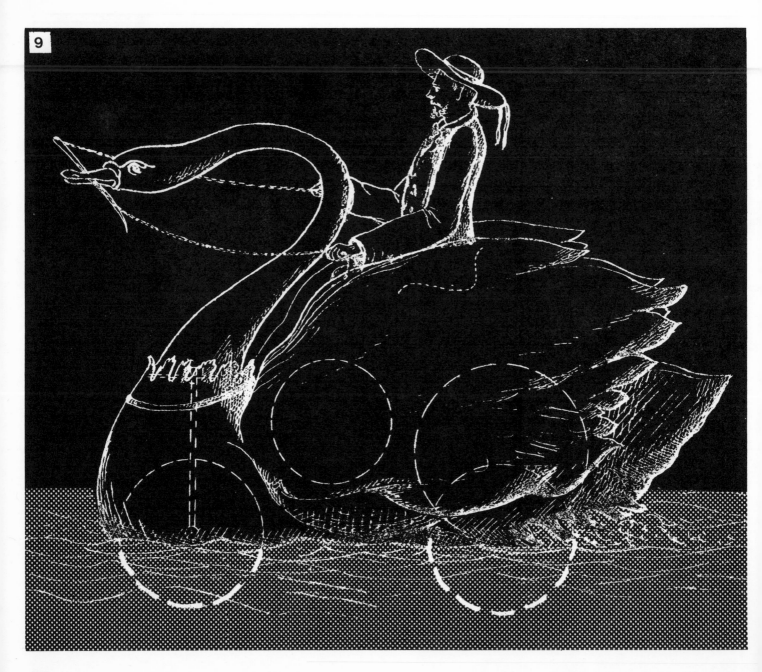

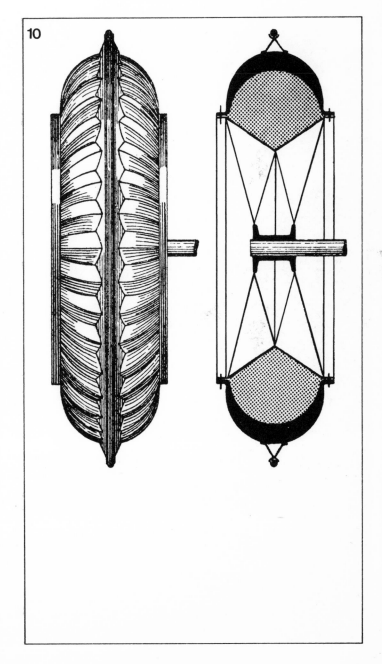

Fig. 10 *Waterwheels patented by Georg Pinkert, Wald-*
heim, Saxony, 1890.

Breslau theatre and as such got his ideas from a production of Wagner's opera *Lohengrin*!

The major problem with these so-called water-velocipedes was undoubtedly the design of the drive wheels. Georg Pinkert of Waldheim in Saxony explains his design, which was patented in 1890 (Fig. 10): The wheel has an inner and an outer chamber so that it remains buoyant even when damaged. Instead of the usual paddles it has a corrugated or ribbed surface to grip the water. In addition there is a narrow outer profile which not only serves as a sort of keel but carries a rubber tread, on which the vehicle rests when travelling on land.

Another invention patented in 1890 by Johannes Breyer of Hamburg, Germany, 'differs from the hitherto known water-velocipedes in that two hollow, high-pitch screws not only propel the vehicle through the water but keep it afloat' (Fig. 11). The two screws are arranged side by side and joined by a framework, which carries the driver and the drive wheel. To achieve an even drive and multiply the driving force, the pedalled wheel is designed as fly-wheel and the power transmitted via a continuous chain to a shaft with a toothed bevel-wheel. On the same shaft two eccentrics diametrically opposed to each other drive the screws via connecting rods.

Muscle power would not seem sufficient to drive this vehicle at any worthwhile speed, but the inventor (as much as eighty years ago!) does suggest that the screws, if suitable gears were installed, *could be driven by a motor.* Anyone wanting to drive an authentic old-timer, if only in facsimile, could do worse than reconstruct this vehicle, which, with the help of modern plastics, should prove neither difficult nor expensive.

Another small paddle-steamer propelled by muscle power came from Hermann Techert of Magdeburg, (now East Germany), in 1893 (Fig. 13). The person driving it sits on a framework between two round floats, which have paddles along the perimeter. These are driven by a foot-operated crank-shaft via an

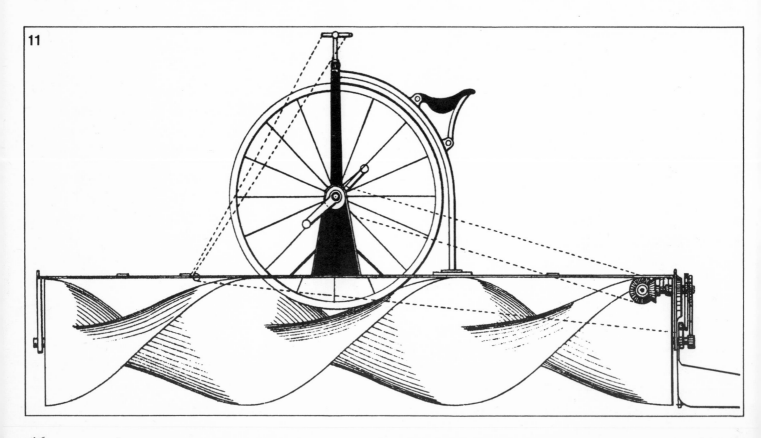

Fig. 12   Water velocipede by Johannes Breyer, Hamburg, 1890 (sectional view).
Fig. 13   Water bicycle with paddlewheel drive by Hermann Teichert, Magdeburg (now East Germany), 1893 (side view).
Fig. 14   Water bicycle with paddlewheel drive by Hermann Teichert, Magdeburg, 1893 (top view). Arrows indicate brake flaps.

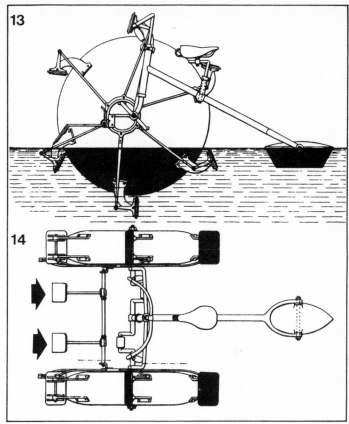

eccentric, which is so positioned that the paddles enter and leave the water almost vertically.

Lateral stability is provided by a small float aft in the position which would otherwise be occupied by a rear wheel (Fig. 14). Another interesting feature are two brake flaps between the paddlewheels. These are pushed into the water by foot pressure, either singly or both together, and can also be used for steering.

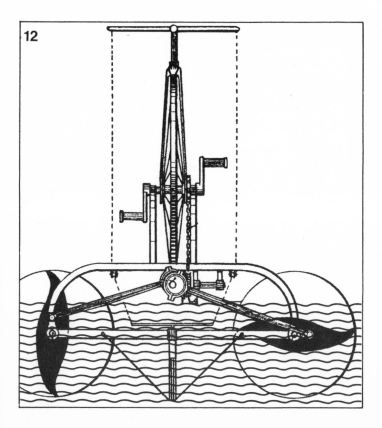

Positively simple by comparison is an apparatus which turned up in 1901 (Fig. 15) and consists of a bicycle mounted on a catamaran. The rear wheel, via a belt drive and rollers, turns a small paddlewheel, which converts the driver's muscular effort into forward propulsion without much delay or resistance. The principle still works today.

A similar idea by Julius Bettinger of Ludwigshafen in Germany, which was patented in 1913, was considerably ahead of its time (Fig. 16). He turned a bicycle or motor bicycle into a water vehicle by mounting it on inflatable floats and had the original idea to make the supports collapsible, so that the parts could be stowed away in an 'inconspicuous' container while the vehicle was used on land.

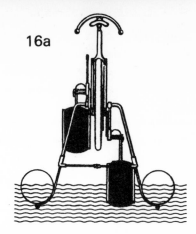

Fig. 15 *Bicycle on catamaran hulls with paddlewheel propulsion. Contemporary illustration, 1901.*

Of notable interest is the use of inflatable floats, which could conveniently be pumped up with the ever-present bicycle pump (or bellows). A batten along the keel line gave them the necessary rigidity. The lids of the containers are removable and are used as the paddles which provide propulsion in the water.

15

Light rubberized fabrics impervious to air did not make their appearance until a decade later. In the inventor's days the floats were made with an inner tube and, for this reason, must have been difficult to use in the intended way, but nowadays, with cycling becoming once again increasingly popular as a leisure and sports activity, this apparatus might well inspire the production of an 'amphibious velocipede'.

When, in 1909, Walter Flexenberger applied for a patent for his 'boat-like bathing apparatus' (Fig. 17) he was not thinking of the basic design, which incorporated a catamaran-type twin hull driven by hand-operated paddlewheels (such features were by then fairly commonplace), nor even of the fact that the sitting and lounging platforms as well as the paddlewheels were adjustable in height for increased efficiency at different loads. The novel feature about his invention was 'two *nets*, one above the other, for sitting and lounging, the upper one of which remains dry and can be pulled out or pushed back rather like a curtain. The upper net is intended for sun-bathing or, when semi-retracted, for foot baths. The lower net is always in the water and can be used like a bathing pool. This means that the user of this bathing craft *can lower himself into his bath and return to his sun-bathing platform without making any adjustments to the craft*. In tropical climates a wire net can be fitted between the floats as protection against reptiles.'

Oh, for the good old cosy days!

Figs. 16a and 16b Water bicycle with paddlewheel propulsion mounted on inflatable hulls by Julius Bettinger, Ludwigshafen, Germany, 1913.

Fig. 17 'Boat-like bathing apparatus' by Walter Flexenberger, 1909.

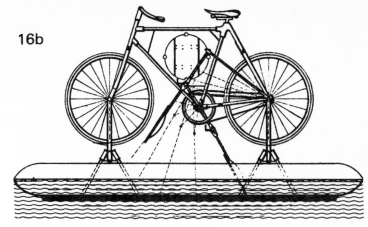

16b

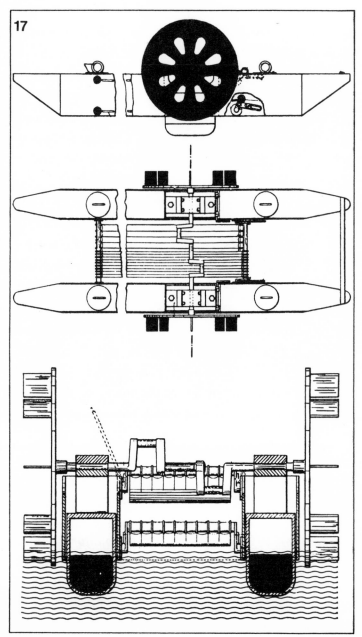

17

The simplest of manual propulsion devices was invented by Franz Xaver Resch of Wanettee, Oklahoma, USA, in 1912 (Fig. 18) and consisted of no more than two wheels with six slim paddles each, which were turned by means of handles. They were mounted on the gunwales. Although paddlewheels had been in use for about a century and paddle steamers had made their appearance and vanished from the scene again, this form of propulsion had never been used on boats, and Resch was granted a patent for his original idea.

As recently as 1929 Artur Kessler of Landshut, in Germany, obtained a patent for his velocipede on paddle-drums (Fig. 19). Upon closer inspection one notices openings in the centre of the paddles, and the inventor explains that: 'in paddlewheels of conventional design each paddle has to lift a column of water as it emerges, and the higher and wider the paddle, the heavier this column of water is. Its sudden collapse causes vibrations which disturb the craft's progress.' Kessler's patented openings or channels allow the air to escape so that the paddles not only emerge from the water more easily but enter it without air bubbles forming. Nevertheless, the fact remains that the craft would have to overcome tremendous resistance due to friction as it moves through the water!

In 1950 Kurt Lipski of Berlin, Germany applied for a patent for something which could be called a trailable tandem paddle-velocipede (Fig. 20). The floats are in sections and together with the paddlewheels and shaft stow in a trailable box. At the water's edge the whole thing is assembled to make a catamaran, in which the trailer box forms the foredeck. The bicycle wheels are removed and paddlewheels are fitted to the rear axle, which is extended outwards for this purpose. The paddlewheels are driven by chains like the original bicycle wheel. For a desk-bound executive in need of physical exercise this would make a suitable appendage to his large motor yacht and at the same time a very handy means of transport for getting to the shops from out-of-the-way anchorages.

The ultimate in ingenuity, however, is the flipper-pedalcraft by Herbert Mende of Bielefeld, Germany,

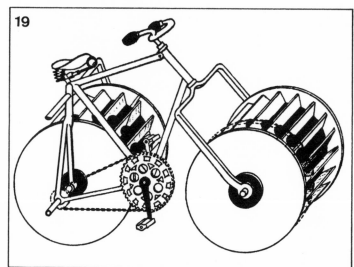

(Fig. 21), for which a patent was applied for in 1955. It recommends itself particularly as space-saving tender, especially for owners of larger yachts who cannot afford an outboard engine but consider rowing below their dignity. One noteworthy feature about this craft was patented separately: the floats, made of light metal, have watertight lids and can be used for stowing provisions and clothing!

This water bicycle, which was first written up in Scientific American in 1855 was invented by the Spaniard Don Ramon Barea. The paddlewheel between the two hulls is set in motion by pedals. 'One cannot quite see', the reporter wrote then, 'why a cyclist cannot remain on dry land to practice his sport and leave the wet element to those who practice the noble sport of rowing and who, by sacred tradition, work it with their hands rather than their feet.'

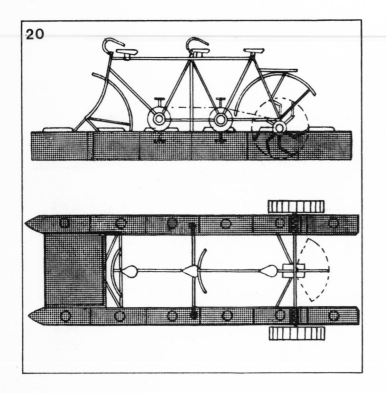

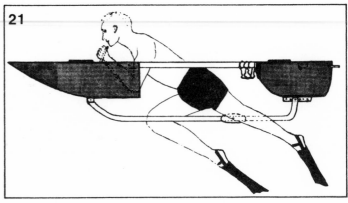

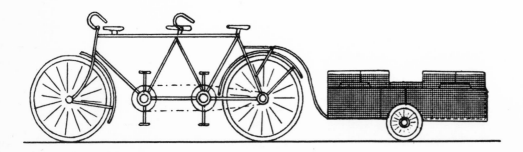

'Scurimobile' was the name given to this water velocipede with hollow screws which, according to reports in contemporary magazines, could be seen afloat in 1896. Five strong men on the pedals were just enough to keep it moving.

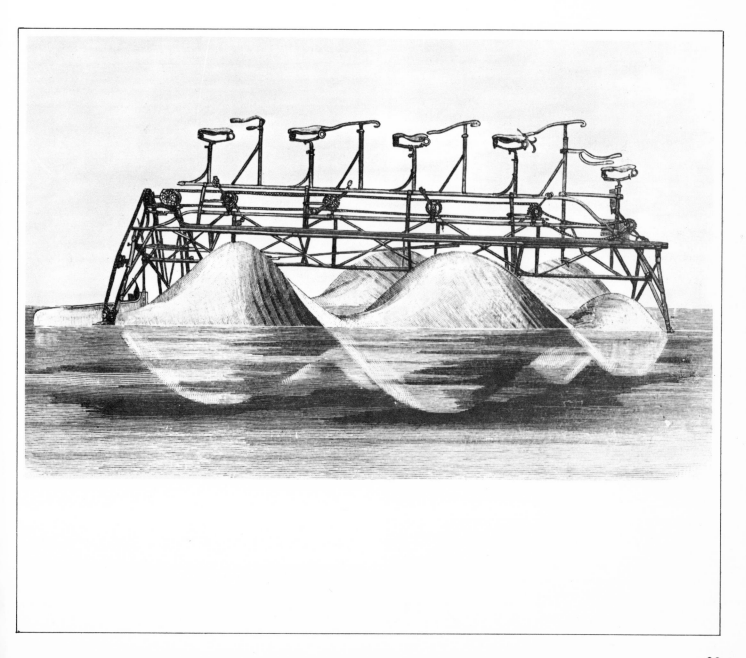

2 Muscle-powered Propeller Drives

Fig. 22 *Hand-operated propeller for small boats by Thomas Reece, Philadelphia, USA, 1866.*
Fig. 23 *Swimming apparatus with propeller operated by stretching the legs, by Johann Andree, East Friesland, Holland, 1881.*

One has to compare the large, clumsy paddlewheel with the relatively small, fast-revolving propeller (then commonly known as ship's screw) in order to appreciate the profound difference between these two forms of propulsion and understand the enthusiasm with which inventors approached the new idea. At the beginning of the nineteenth century many types and sizes of propellers were developed exclusively for merchant shipping until, in 1866, Thomas Reece of Philadelphia, USA, hit upon the idea of seeking a

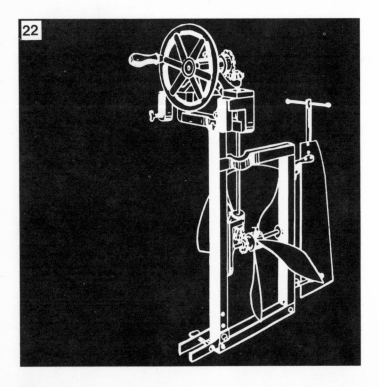

patent for his 'hand operated propeller for whalers, yawls, pleasure boats, skiffs and similar craft which so far have normally been propelled by oars and small sails' (Fig. 22). Many people followed his lead in designing propeller-driven swimming devices which hardly deserve to be called boats, right up to the kind of lifeboat, still in use today, in which a number of oarsmen turn the propeller shaft by hand.

In 1881 a Dutchman from East Friesland, Johann Andree, invented a device consisting of a hollow, watertight buoyancy tank made of wood or sheet metal, which was fastened to the user's back with straps. The designer particularly aimed at optimum effort utilization and minimum resistance: 'The forward end of the tank is streamlined for manoeuvrability and to enable it to slice through the waves.' To make sure that the user is comfortable on his float it is

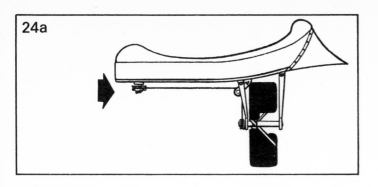

24a

Figs. 24a and 24b Swimming machine with propeller attached to a buoyant seat, by Johann Andree, 1881.
Figs. 25a and 25b Swimming apparatus with ship's screw by Ludwig Bauhofer, Munich, Germany, 1890 (side and top view).

upholstered with a sea-grass mattress. The propeller on the underside is made to rotate in alternate directions by foot-operated ropes (Fig. 24). So that the float will always move forward, the propeller blades are made to turn through approximately 90°, as far as their retaining pins, every time the propeller rotation is reversed. It seems that we have here the prototype of the feathering propeller.

In the 'swimming apparatus with screw propeller' which Ludwig Bauhofer of Munich, Germany invented in 1890 (Fig. 26) the driver lies in an adjustable harness between two streamlined hollow floats (Fig. 27). His leg effort is transmitted, via pedals and gears, to a twin-bladed propeller. Steering is by means of a handle-bar, to which the rudder blade is attached.

The following designs, all of them aimed at 'enabling swimmers and non-swimmers alike to spend longer periods on the water and move over longer distances

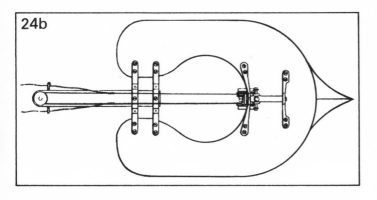

24b

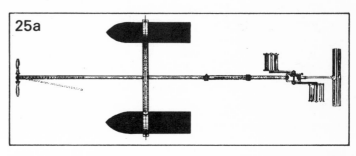

25a

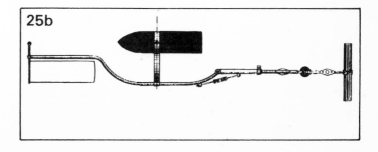

25b

Not quite as comfortable was the hand-and-foot-operated swimming apparatus which William Richardson of Alabama, USA, invented in 1880 (Fig. 25). However, it offered less resistance and is said to have reached the astounding maximum speed of 3 knots.

25

Fig. 26   Swimming apparatus with ship's screw by Ludwig Bauhofer of Munich, 1890 (sectional view).

26

without considerable physical effort' interest us only in so far as they represent a gradual transition to the type of boat we know today. All of them reflect man's desire for travel and diversion on the water, but up until the appearance of light materials and small marine engines there remained a wide discrepancy between dream and reality, as is obvious from these inventions right up to the thirties. Not until then could the would-be mariners among our parents and grand-parents exchange their watery contraptions for the comfort of a dry hull.

Figs. 28 and 29 show an apparatus devised by Joseph Tichy of Vienna, Austria, in 1898. It is a compact unit consisting of a hand-operated propeller on a short shaft and a float with sufficient buoyancy to keep one's moustache above water.

The machine designed in Germany by Czeslaw Jedynecki of Berlin in 1912 (Figs 30 and 31) is propelled not by pedalling but by moving the legs sideways as one does when swimming breast-stroke. The user is surrounded by floats and by his leg action displaces the bar sideways 'similar to the principle on which a drill

Fig. 28   Propeller-driven swimming machine by Joseph Tichy of Vienna, Austria, 1895 (sectional view).

Fig. 29   Propeller-driven swimming machine by Joseph Tichy of Vienna, 1895 (side view).

Fig. 30   Propeller-driven swimming apparatus by Czeslaw Jedynecki of Berlin, 1912 (side view).

Fig. 31   Propeller-driven swimming apparatus by Czeslaw Jedynecki of Berlin, 1912 (close-up).

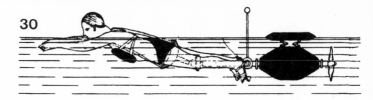

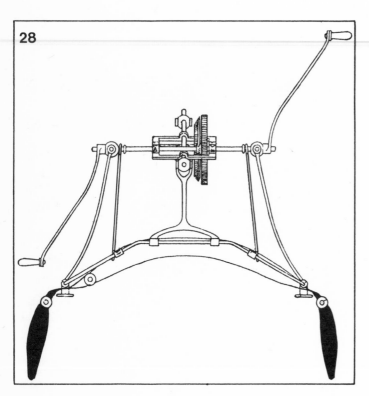

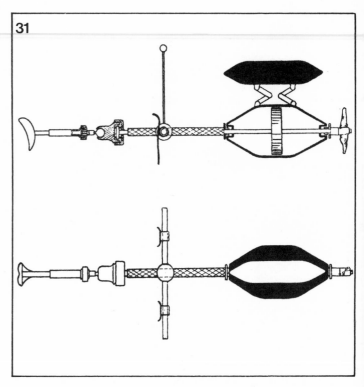

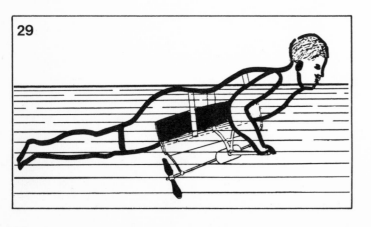

works'. The propeller sits at the end of a shaft, which passes through a fly-wheel encased in a watertight housing and has both a left- and a right-handed thread, so that the propeller always turns in the same direction. The inventor does not say whether his apparatus is intended to teach people the leg action in breast-stroke swimming, nor does he disperse any doubts one might have over whether the proposed leg effort is sufficient to overcome the considerable friction inside the mechanism and actually drive the propeller.

Fig. 32 Hand-and-foot-driven swimming machine by René Gustave Chaligné of Paris, 1927 (side view).

Fig. 33 Hand-and-foot-propelled swimming machine by René Gustave Chaligné of Paris, 1927 (top view).

Fig. 34 Flotation collar with manual drive by Ernst Huboldt of Berlin, 1929 (side view).

Fig. 35 Flotation collar by Ernst Huboldt of Berlin, 1929 (detail).

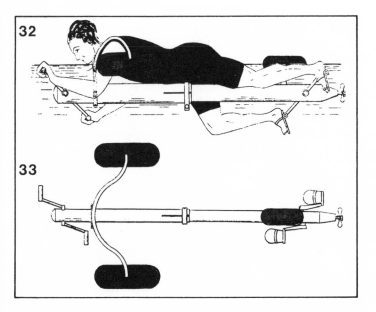

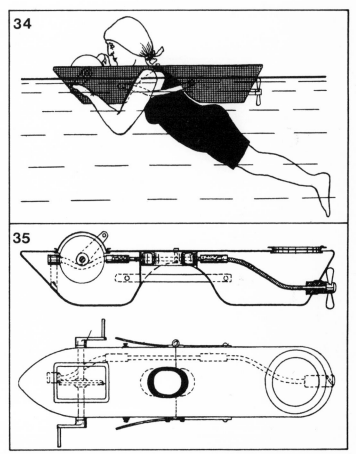

René Gustave Chaligné of Paris was particularly concerned with the telescopic parts of his swimming apparatus (Figs 32 and 33) when he had it patented in 1927. Compared with the device illustrated in Figs 26 and 27 its advantage seems to lie mainly in the fact that the distance between handle bar and foot pedals can be adjusted to suit the particular user by means of a telescopic tube connecting the two. It could hardly have been very comfortable, especially for gentlemen, to lie for any length of time on the clamp ring which holds the rear tube inside the slotted forward tube.

Something which might be called a flotation collar was invented by Ernst Huboldt of Berlin, Germany in 1929 (Fig. 34). The body of this 'boat' is made up of several sections and has an opening in the middle to allow the head to pass through. The user turns the propeller at the end of a flexible shaft by means of a handle immediately in front of his nose.

29

Fig. 36   Swimming machine by Alphonse Daydé, France, 1926 (side view).

Fig. 37   Swimming machine by Alphonse Daydé, France, 1926 (top view).

Fig. 38   Swimming machine with cuddy and propeller drive by Henry Thubeauville, Düsseldorf, Germany, 1919.

Fig. 39   Pedal-propelled swimming machine by Max Weiszflog, 1921 (adjusted for lying down).

Fig. 40   Pedal-propelled swimming machine by Max Weiszflog, 1921 (adjusted for sitting up).

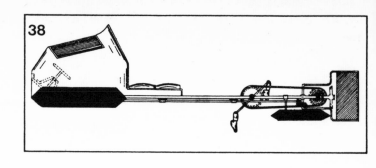

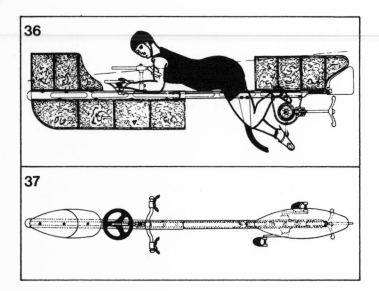

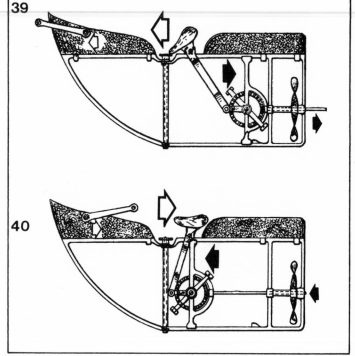

The swimming machine patented by the Frenchman Alphonse Daydé in 1926 had so much buoyancy that a large part of it remained above water (Figs 36 and 37). Although in itself it was narrow, the buoyancy compartments at the stern as well as underneath and in front of the user were of considerable size. The wheel steering is well worth examination.

In 1919 Henri Thubeauville of Dusseldorf, Germany, invented a vehicle (Fig. 38) the outstanding feature of which is the cuddy to protect the user from wind, rain and spray—an absurd idea when one considers that the person was practically immersed in the water anyway! But now things were looking up, even though the apparatus designed by Max Weiszflog in 1921 did not

float quite as high in the water as the drawing might suggest. One particularly interesting feature of this design becomes apparent only upon closer inspection: the saddle and the handle-bar can be used in two positions so that the user can either *lie* on the machine with the handle-bar folded forward (Fig. 39), or he can sit on it with the handle-bar folded aft and the pedal wheel shifted forward (Fig. 40).

Fig. 41 Hand-propelled motor sailer by Francois Bara-thon, France, 1895.

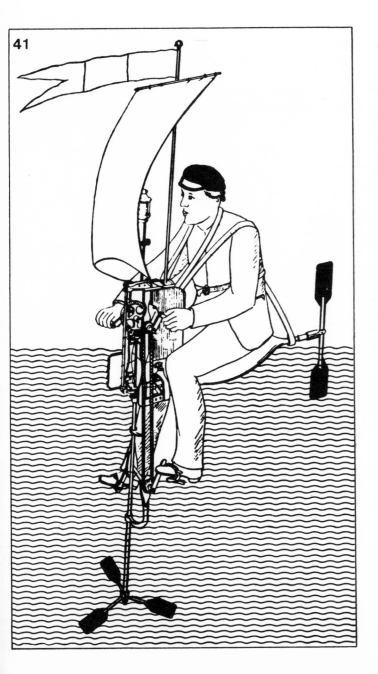

41

The first hand-operated motor-sailer was designed in 1895 by the Frenchman Francois Barathon (Fig. 41). What is more, we have here what amounts to an inflatable boat, for the single-handed skipper sits on an air-pillow. In its day the machine was intended as a modern life-saving device. The shipwrecked mariner had to inflate the air-pillow and throw the whole apparatus into the water, whereupon, securely lashed to it, he hurriedly made for the safety of land by driving the propeller at the stern by means of handles and foot pedals. The additional propeller on the underside, which turns horizontally, was obviously designed to provide further buoyancy. In a following wind he could set a square sail, but he had to take this down again as soon as shipping approached, so that he could send out morse signals with the lamp immediately in front of him. Obviously a machine of great versatility!

If one ignores the openings for arms and legs which, of course, have to be immersed in the water with this type of propulsion by muscular effort, the 'boat-like swimming apparatus' (Figs 42 and 43) by Markus Sembach of Thuringen, Germany (1922) could almost be called the forerunner of our present-day dinghy with built-in buoyancy. It consists of a hollow, boat-shaped, watertight body with air chambers and openings for the legs, which drive a propeller via bevelled cogwheels, and for the arms, which do the steering.

We must not fail to include in this selection a

Fig. 42 'Boat-like swimming apparatus' by Markus Sembach from Thuringia, Austria, 1922 (side view).

Fig. 43 'Boat-like swimming apparatus' by Markus Sembach, Thuringia, 1922 (top view).

Fig. 44 Boat propelled by muscle power by Christian Petersen, Hamburg, 1897 (top and side view).

Fig. 45 Boat propelled by muscle power by Christian Petersen, Hamburg, 1897 (section).

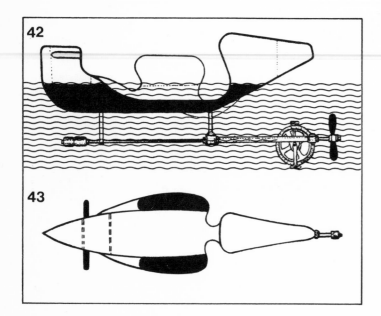

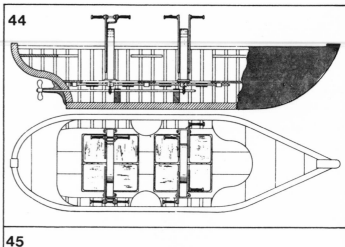

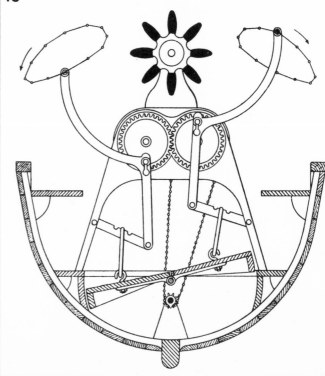

muscle-driven propeller which was patented as early as 1897 by Christian Petersen of Hamburg, Germany and is still used on lifeboats today (Fig. 44). The transmission is driven by one pair or several pairs of foot pedals and hand levers simultaneously (Fig.45). In other words, it is the combined hand and foot effort which, via a chain drive, drives the propeller shaft.

We have now progressed to the point where our mariner at least sits above the water, but the following

Fig. 46   Pedalcraft by Martin Egerland, Munich, 1917
Fig. 47a and 47b   Pinafore by A. E. Tangen of Bismarck,
Dakota, USA, 1879.

47a & b

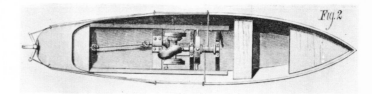

vehicle by Martin Egerland of Munich (1917) still offers very little in the way of protection. It is made up of two floats which pivot round a vertical axis and are supposed to have adequate buoyancy (Fig. 46). 'Whereas all hitherto known water vehicles of this type get their stability from the width of the part immersed in the water, this craft is stabilized by lateral displacement of the centre of gravity. This makes it possible to keep both the width and displacement of the craft to the minimum and thereby not only make it light and easy to manoeuvre but capable of reaching high speeds in relation to the propulsive force required.'

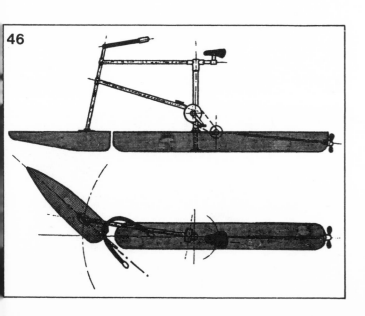

46

Such considerations concerning the weight of muscle-operated vessels were then new and no doubt commendable, and they also show why all inventions of this type were doomed to failure in the end. This particular craft was bound to lack the necessary stability to move across smooth water, let alone rough water.

The *Pinafore* by A.E. Tangen of Bismarck, Dakota, USA, (Fig. 47), on the other hand, did not pose any problems as to its inherent stability but is hardly likely

48

to have made much headway with an output of about 1/4 hp because of its weight.

Good progress, by comparison was made by the users of H.B. Ogden's (of New York, USA), light marine-tandem in 1893. It was decked fore and aft and was used as a training machine for competition crews of rowing boats (Fig. 50)

As early as 1894 one could enjoy a promenade on the river Havel in Berlin in a boat propelled by three men doing some energetic work with foot pedals (Fig. 49). They are reported to have reached speeds as high as 5 knots.

50a & 50b

Fig. 51 Propeller operated by foot levers by Walter Forward, San Diego, USA, 1895.

Fig. 52 Hand-operated outboard motor by Christian Krohn, New York, 1911.

Efforts by two Americans, Michael Batz of Brooklyn in 1884 and by Walter Forward of San Diego in 1895, to develop a boat with hand-lever propulsion (Fig. 48) or combined hand-lever and foot-propulsion (Fig. 51) respectively never led to anything useful. The contemporary illustration, Fig. 51, depicts a rushing bow wave, but it is extremely doubtful whether the complicated machinery of flywheels and drive belts ever managed to turn the propeller, let alone shift the boat.

Another entry in the golden book of international patents concerns the first hand-operated outboard motor (Fig. 52) designed by Christian Krohn of New York. Although in those days a number of remarkable outboard motors were already in existence (these are described in detail in Chapter 6), there was not one which consisted of a propeller on a hand-operated shaft

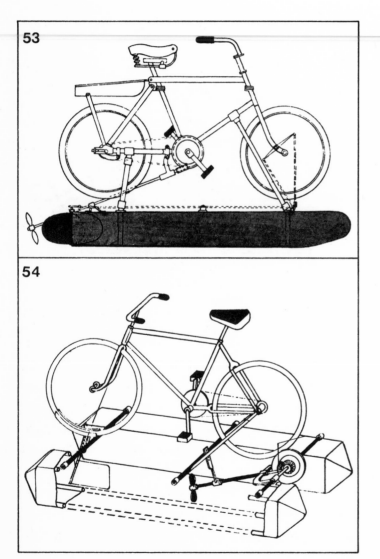

53

54

secured to the transom. Krohn was given a patent for it in 1911 after having already been granted one for a similar hand-operated propulsion device for use by a person wearing a life-jacket.

Meanwhile the bicycle brigade zealously pursued their efforts somehow to use the typical pedal action of the bicycle for driving a propeller. As recently as 1948 Leopold Fuksa of Rio Grande do Sul in Brazil was given a patent on his design shown in Fig. 53. In it the shaft is driven by a cogwheel mounted on the side of the bicycle chain, and the rudder between the two floats is operated by the handle-bar via a yoke. Of course, all the parts and fastenings besides the floats can be carried on the bicycle, so that we have here a truly modern amphibious vehicle. Fig. 54 illustrates how very slight differences qualify for a separate patent. The inventors, Alfred and Otto Zacke of Southern Germany, mounted a bicycle rigidly on floats, had the propeller shaft driven by the rear wheel via a friction disc and hoped that the propeller, even at this unfavourable angle, would manage to move the craft against the current. The rudder was at the forward end and was operated directly by the handle-bar of the bicycle.

The ideal solution has yet to be found!

3 The First Motorboat –Daimler and His Competitors

Patent No. 36367 registered by the German Gottlieb Daimler on 9 October 1886, concerning 'an installation for driving a ship's screw by means of a gas or petrol/paraffin motor' already features all the usual elements of an inboard engine such as reverse gear and cooling system. Its significance then and now can only be fully appreciated in contrast with all the fantastic and impracticable designs which were patented at the same time but never went into production, or only for a short time.

The gas or petrol/paraffin engine turns the crankshaft at a constant speed and always in the same direction. Clutch plates and bevelled wheels provide a gear mechanism with which the propeller can be made to drive the ship either forward or in reverse. Figs 56 and 57 show a further remarkable detail, which has remained unchanged to the present day: the cooling of the working cylinder by sea water. The cooling water is pressed into the tube at the forward end and sucked out at the after end, where there is a one-way valve. To increase the efficiency of the cooling system a centrifugal pump is mounted on the driving shaft, which aids this process. A three-way tap ensures that the water passes from the sea, or the bilges, to the pump or to the water jacket of the cylinder.

A further patent covers the crank handle, which is coupled to the crank shaft and is used to start the engine.

When the motor is run on gas, the gas cylinders serve

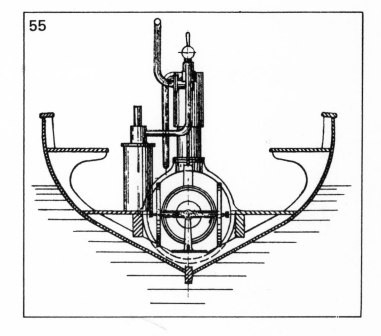

Fig. 55 Gas or petrol/paraffin motor patented by Gottlieb Daimler in 1886 as installed in a boat (section).

the additional purpose of making the boat unsinkable. The gas is stowed in high-pressure containers secured under the side benches (Fig. 57). From there the gas is made to flow (either by hand or through a reducing valve) to the low-pressure tanks in the bilges, from where it supplies the engine.

The patent contains an interesting remark concerning the utilization of the exhaust gases: 'The exhaust gases, which leave the engine under pressure, are expelled in the opposite direction to that in which the vessel moves, so that they help to propel the vessel by jet effect.'

The first trial runs with Daimler's motorboat took

Fig. 56   Gas or petrol/paraffin motor patented by Gottlieb Daimler in 1886 as installed in a boat (side and top view).

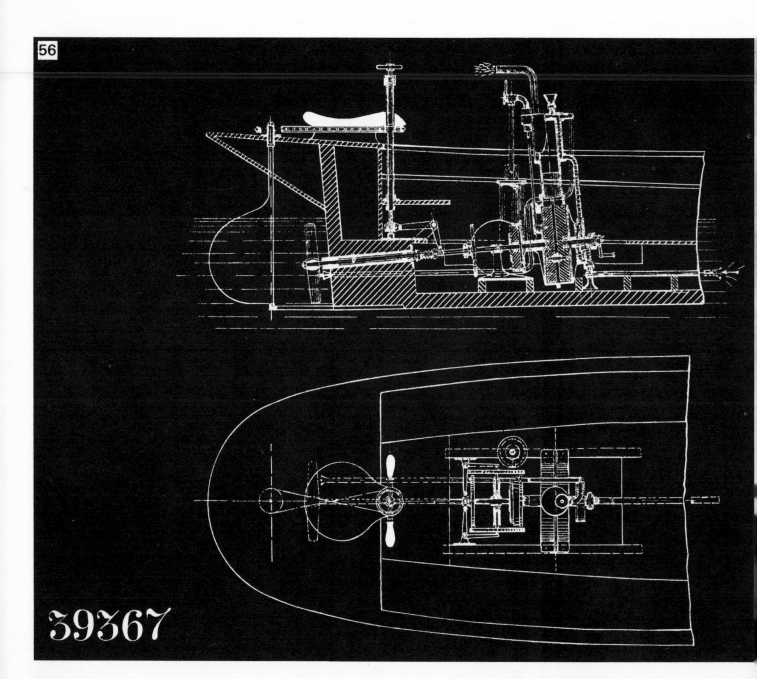

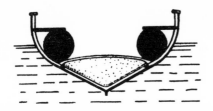

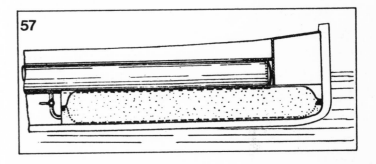

place in August 1886. In October of the same year it was first shown to government officials. In 1888 a similar boat named *Maria* was presented to Bismarck. This can still be seen in a museum. When, on 15 October 1888, an engine of the same type was demonstrated on the River Elbe in Germany, the 23 ft boat, named *The Seven Suabians*, with its 2 hp motor running at 740 rpm caused quite a stir.

It was part of a cortège of tugs which accompanied Kaiser Wilhelm II on his inspection trip of the new port of Hamburg. Not only did it surprise people, but it had them wondering what fuel was driving it. Many who noticed the absence of a chimney and a stoker thought it was an electric motor and possibly another invention by Edison, who was very much in the headlines just then.

This episode in Germany had its effect on developments in other countries. In 1891 trial runs were held on the River Thames in London before a group of motorboat enthusiasts, who were mainly interested in the commercial potential of this new invention in improving harbour traffic.

The use of petrol as a fuel was viewed with great misgivings, because of its explosive nature, and people's fears were not confined to fast sports cars on land.

But let us return to this the most important invention of its time. Daimler's fuel was not only explosive and hence dangerous, but the motor and its whole installa-tions were rather heavy and not by any means as efficient as internal combustion engines are today. It weighed approximately 130 lbs, developed 1.5 hp and gave the boat a speed of 5 knots.

A direct conversion of energy had been proposed in 1790 by the American John Fitch (Fig. 58). Water flowed through a pipe from the bow of the boat via a one-way valve to a boiler, where it was heated. When a certain pressure had been reached this valve was pushed open, and the water flowed out at the stern. As the boiler cooled down a vacuum formed in it, which sucked in fresh water from the bow. The constant repetition of this process was supposed to move the boat forward.

Although the idea was based on the correct physical principles, the necessary energy source was not avail-able in those days. We have it now in the shape of atomic energy, and perhaps the flow of water could even be made to drive a propeller, which would provide the necessary push. Another example of a basically sound idea which could not be realized with the means available at the time. Could it be made to work today?

In 1898 Herman F.L. Linden of Naples, Italy, had a boat patented, which was propelled by wave motion. Before him Carl G. Henning had received a patent for a similar invention in 1874. Both inventors sought to utilize the not inconsiderable energy contained in the

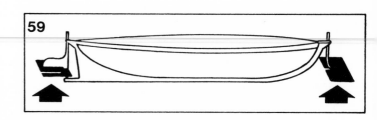

long and was fitted with two fins. These were 20 in wide and 10 in deep, 0.08 in thick at the forward edge and 0.02 in thick at the after edge. At the after edge they had a number of horizontal slots. When the boat was in motion they moved with the waves and propelled the boat forward. According to reports the *Autonaut* reached a speed of 3 knots against wind and sea. The largest of Linden's boats, which was 24 ft long, even reached 4 knots.

When Peter Beckmann introduced his 'roller boat' in 1898 (Fig. 60), he, too, made use of the kinetic energy of the waves. It consisted of a cylinder approximately 9 ft 10 in in diameter and 11 ft 6 in long, on the outside of which was fitted a framework of beams. Its interior served as cabin, and round it there revolved a pair of paddlewheels, which were moved by the waves. Peter Beckmann of Bar Harbor, Maine, USA, and his son took this boat along the American coast and 15 miles out into the Atlantic at a speed of about 7 knots. The leeway made was so great, however, that they asked a freighter for a lift to New York.

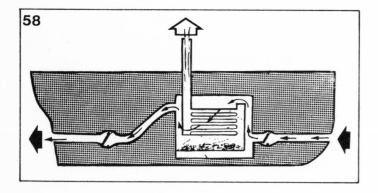

orbital motion of waves, which is as freely available to motorboats all over the world's oceans as the wind is to sailing boats. Linden tried to extract a small part of that energy and use flexible fins to convert it into forward motion of the boat (Fig. 59).

The first boat by Linden, named *Autonaut*, was 13 ft

Fig. 60   Roller boat by Peter Beckmann, 1898.

60

Fig. 61 *Centrifugal drive by steam injection. Patent by Alfred Leon Segond, Paris, 1884.*

Fig. 62 *Compressed air motor in a lifeboat by Kurt Fronhöfer, Schwerin (now East Germany), 1889 (side view).*

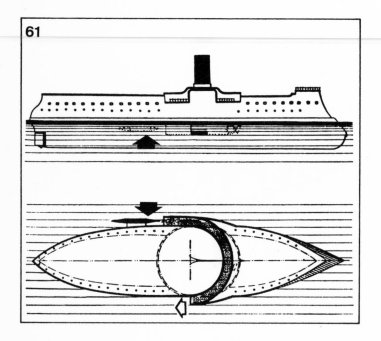

61

The idea of moving a boat without a propeller also occurred to the Frenchman Alfred Leon Segond of Paris in 1884, only in his case the vessel was a rather big ship (Fig. 61). He was given a patent for his steam injection pump, which was to push water round a semi-circular tube installed horizontally in the ship. Segond believed that the ship would be moved forward by centrifugal force, but his idea did not work.

The pneumatic motor for a lifeboat patented in 1889 (Figs 62 and 63) can be classed as a curiosity. The boat consisted of two independent parts; an airtight forward part, in which provisions, ballast etc. were to be carried, and the after part, in which there was room for the crew. The two parts were linked by strong, hinge-like couplings, which allowed the forward part to move up and down in a seaway. This pitching

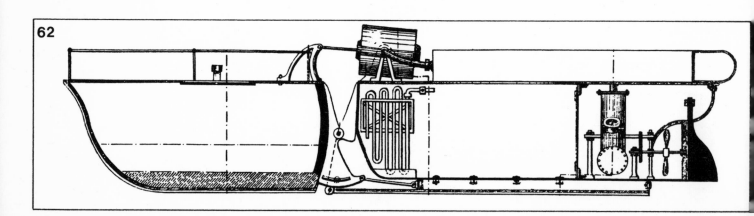

62

Fig. 63 Compressed air motor in a lifeboat by Kurt Fronhöfer, Schwerin, 1889 (sections).

Figs 64a and 64b Drive by liquid carbon-dioxide as patented by Bruno von Livonius, Stuttgart, 1904.

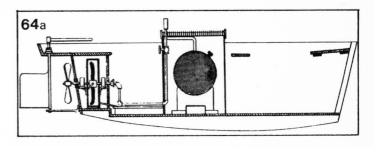

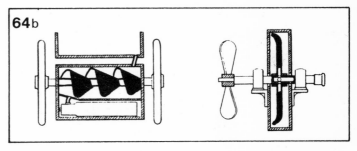

motion was to activate two compression pumps, and the compressed air produced in this way was to drive the propeller. For use in calm waters, when the pitching motion would be lacking, containers with compressed air (40-50 atmospheres) were to be carried on board.

Another drive mechanism based on compressed air was that by Bruno Livonius of Stuttgart, Germany, invented in 1904 (Figs 64a and 64b). It used liquid carbon-dioxide, which was fed into a reaction wheel coupled to the propeller shaft. The carbon-dioxide was stored in special containers, and as it left the jets became gasified. After use it was recovered, liquefied once again and re-used.

Lightness and safety were the main features of this invention. 'Compared to steam engines or other motors the use of carbon-dioxide has the advantage that it excludes any fire risk. This makes this type of propulsion particularly suitable for racing yachts, racing boats and similar craft in which low weight and safe operation are of primary importance.'

With larger internal combustion engines an ordinary crank handle was not usually powerful enough to turn and start the engine, and the use of a larger starting handle was rarely possible in the confined space of most engine rooms. With this in mind the German gas-motor manufacturers of Deutz applied for a patent

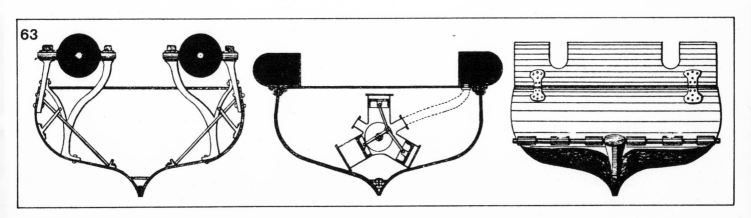

Fig. 65 Underwater jet propulsion by Ernest Morice, France, 1921.

Fig. 66 Propulsion by compressed air or gas by Henri Arnold Johannes de Beijll Nachenius, Haarlem, Holland, 1922.

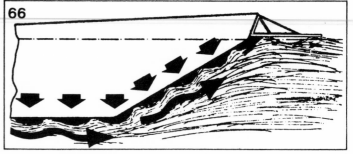

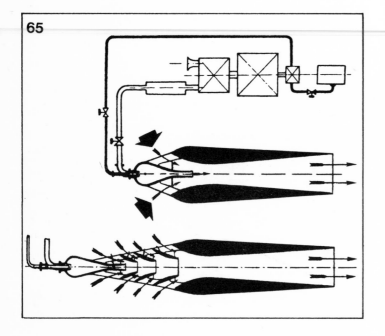

for an invention which was to facilitate the starting of the engine: the drive shaft of the engine could be engaged with and disengaged from the steering column by a clutch, so that the motor could be started by turning the steering wheel.

A special form of underwater jet propulsion was patented in 1921 by the Frenchman Ernest Morice of Boulogne-sur-Seine (Fig. 65). In the combustion chamber liquid fuel is mixed with oxygen, and as the ignited gas leaves the chamber at high speed this

produces low pressure, which sucks in water at one end. As soon as the kinetic energy of the gas has passed into the water the latter, with reduced pressure, flows out through the enlarged after opening of the main jet.

The Dutchman Henri Arnold Johannes de Beijll Nachenius of Haarlem had an old invention patented in 1922 (Fig. 66). His boat was propelled by compressed air or gas, which emerged through openings on the keel line. As it travelled along the upward-slanting stern of the boat, it caused the water to vibrate and accelerate along the stern.

A similar type of jet propulsion was patented in 1949 by Fritz Zwicky of Pasadena, California, USA, (Fig. 67). Three liquids are fed into a reactor: water, a reagent and a detergent. The water and the reagent are injected separately into the jet and mixed, while the detergent is injected into a branched jet. The reaction

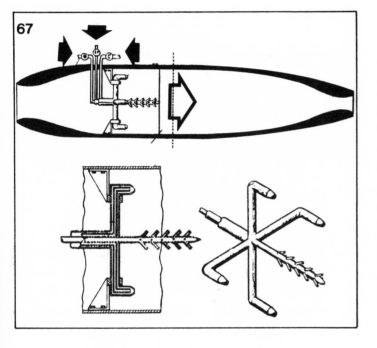

'cooling system and cooling device for ships' combustion engines' which uses the principles of our modern dual-circuit cooling (Fig. 68). It uses the thermo-syphon cooling system usual in land-operated combustion engines and for economy does away with cooling-water pumps.

The cooling-water tank is in the forepeak and is either in direct contact with the hull skin, which in turn is cooled by the sea, or the hull skin itself forms the sides of the cooling tank. The engine cylinder is linked by pipes to this heat exchanger, which gives off the heat of the cooling water to the water-cooled skin of the hull.

In 1938 Hermann Waimer of Friedrichshafen in Germany invented the actual modern dual-circuit cooling system, in which the water of the inner cooling circuit,

between the water and the reagent accelerates the flow of water and propels at least the jet and its fuel containers in a forward direction. It seems unlikely that the reaction is powerful enough to propel a boat and its load at a useful speed.

Before very long the problem of corrosion caused by seawater-cooling of marine engines led to efforts to improve cooling systems. In 1922 Julius Loewy of Königsberg in Germany, was given a patent for a

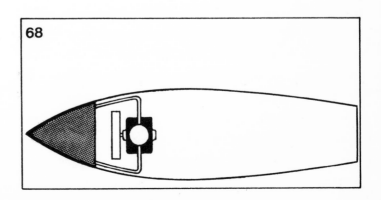

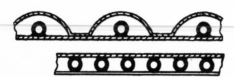

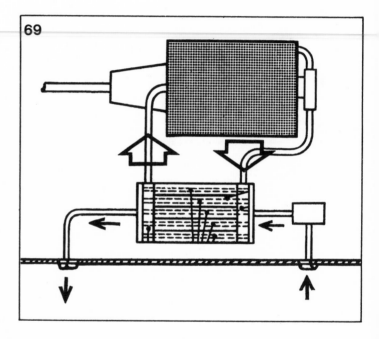

enclosed in thin pipes, passes through a heat exchanger, through which sea water is pumped in a separate, enclosed system (Fig. 69). This invention was a great improvement on the previously described system, in which the heat exchange through the hull skin was inadequate. It also ensures efficient cooling while the boat moves at low speeds or not at all. Even in recent times efforts have been continued to develop an efficient 'muscle-power motor' as an alternative to the costly internal combustion engine. In 1949 Emil Mayer of Munich had patented a pedal-propulsion system, in which the foot-pedal action drives a side-mounted outboard motor and its propeller shaft. When touching ground the propeller shaft tilts up (Fig. 70).

An engineer from Frankfurt, Germany, Erich Feist, thought of using hand and foot action for operating air or liquid pumps and using the compressed air or compressed liquid for driving the boat (Fig. 71). In a sitting position the skipper bends and stretches his left and right leg alternately and in doing so operates the two pumps, which pass compressed air via a tank into a compressed-air turbine, which drives the propeller.

Another member of the muscle-power brigade was Alwin Franz of Hanau, Germany, whose idea it was to

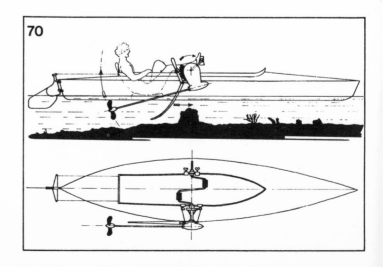

Fig. 71   Propeller driven by foot-operated air- and liquid-pumps by Erich Feist, Frankfurt, Germany, 1950.
Fig. 72   Hand-operated outboard motor by Alwin Franz, Hanau, Germany, 1950.

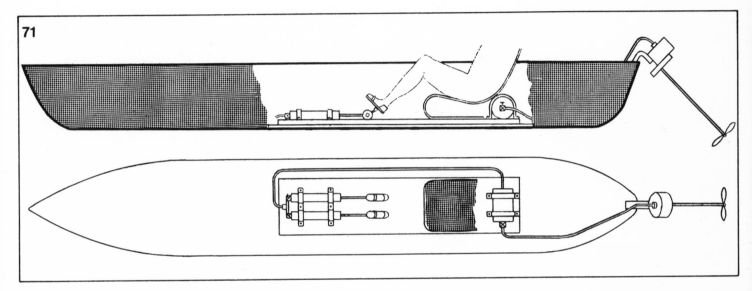

turn an outboard propeller by pulling at a recoiling rope wound round the propeller shaft (Fig. 72). The principle is better illustrated in Fig. 73, where it is used in a swimming apparatus. The rope, which is unwound as the swimmer's legs are stretched, or as the body of the person in the boat is bent back, returns to its original position as the legs are drawn up or, in the case of the boat, the body is bent forward.

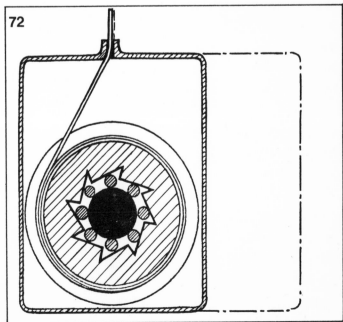

Fig. 73 Propeller driven by leg-stretching by Alwin Franz, Hanau, 1950.

Fig. 74 Boat with foot-operated jet propulsion by Erich Feist, Frankfurt, Germany, 1951.

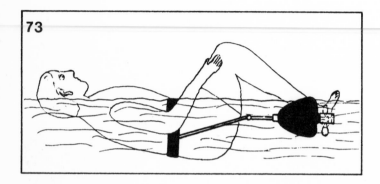

In 1951 Erich Feist of Frankfurt was granted a patent for his muscle-propelled leisure boat (Fig. 74), in which the driver moves both arms and legs to operate fluid pumps. The compressed fluid here is used to propel the craft in a different manner: under the floor

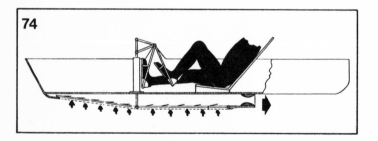

on either side there is a long pump chamber, into which water flows from below as the pedals are operated. The flaps are then closed, and as the water is ejected through a jet aft so the boat moves forward.

Our examples show how narrow the borderline is between fantastic dreams and workable realities. But most inventors are amateurs, who lack the know-how to see their ideas through, even if they had the necessary financial resources. This is often done by other people, who lack the creative genius but know how to handle production and marketing. Only very few people combine both abilities, one of them was undoubtedly Gottlieb Daimler.

No doubt, efforts will continue in future both to improve conventional methods of boat propulsion and invent new ones. Fortunately the history of technology shows that every principle, however perfected it seems, is not only worth improving but actually capable of improvement. Fortunately I say, for what would man be if he had no scope for creative thought and inventive activity?

As long ago as 1910 motorboat races were held on the *Müggelsee near Berlin. This is* Daimler I *giving an impressive demonstration of Gottlieb Daimler's internal combustion engine.*

4 The Thrill of Planing

Fig. 75 Planing hull by Raoul Pierre Pictet, Geneva, Switzerland, 1881.

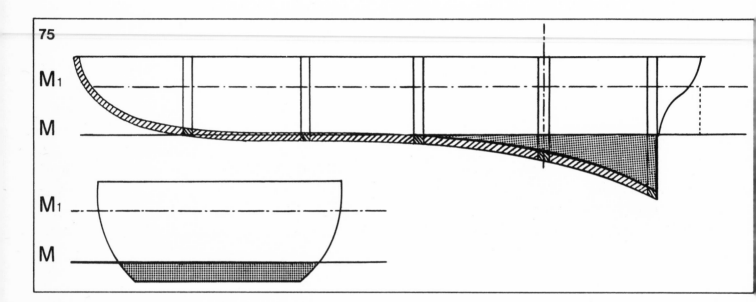

Nowadays planing boats are taken for granted, and it is hard to imagine that not so long ago boat designers and owners knew nothing of the principles of hydrodynamic lift and were ignorant of the shape of a planing hull. They only had the vaguest idea of such possibilities, and therefore their experiments were very much hit-and-miss. 'The ship-hulls hitherto built are based on the Archimedean principle,' writes Raoul Pierre Pictet of Geneva, Switzerland, in 1881 in his patent specification entitled *New trends in ships' hulls.* 'They displace an amount of water exactly equal to their own weight, and different speeds change only imperceptibly the immersed hull area. In order to reach high speeds . . . one has designed boats with slim keels and pointed ends, whose greatest beam coincides roughly with the midship frame. My new design is based on the Archimedean principle in combination with a dynamic principle, which results in the boat moving with greater ease and at higher speeds.'

Raoul Pictet thus appears to have been the first designer to propose a hull which, when at rest or moving slowly, was deeply immersed with the waterline at M1, but at greater speeds was lifted higher up in the water thanks to its special shape, so that the waterline moved to M (Fig. 75).

In fact his design was that of a flat-bottomed planing hull which was only slightly curved downwards towards the stern, since the propeller shaft of the inboard engine had somehow to pass through the hull. Of course, this planing hull shape does not stand up to

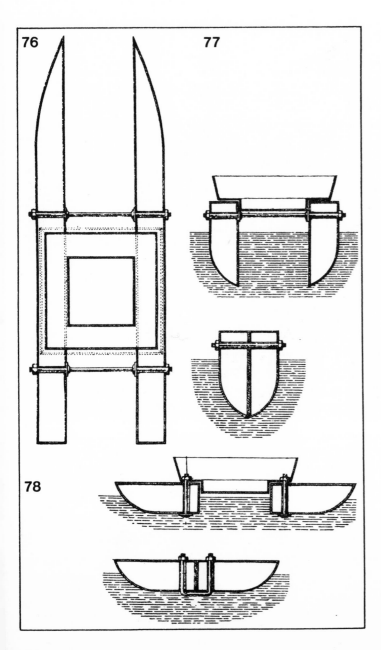

Fig. 76   Early catamaran by Claudius Damond, Paris, 1889 (top view).
Fig. 77   Catamaran by Claudius Damond, Paris, 1889. Hulls arranged for deep draught and as single-hulled boat.
Fig. 78   Catamaran by Claudius Damond, Paris, 1889. Hulls arranged for shallow draught and as single-hulled boat.

modern criteria, but Pictet had already realized that to move a boat from a standstill 'the steam in the cylinder would have to be raised', but once a certain speed had been reached this could be maintained even by a reduced engine output. In other words, as early as 1881 the Swiss designer had recognized the difference between a displacement hull and a planing hull: the displacement hull needs to overcome wave resistance whereas the planing hull rises up and thus reduces resistance.

A lot of subsequent experiments would have been unnecessary if the 'water-borne vessel consisting of two separate hulls' which Claudius Damond of Paris had patented in 1898 had not been dismissed in its day as futuristic (Fig. 76). In fact we can recognize in it not only an early forerunner of our catamarans but a logical design, which might be worth reviving. The two hulls are so shaped that they make up a deep-draught (i.e. displacement) hull if they are joined one way (Fig. 77) and a shallow-draught planing hull if they are joined the other way (Fig. 78). The only thing missing was a lightweight outboard engine, and so this invention remained theory. There was no room in this catamaran to install the only available marine engine, i.e. Gottlieb Daimler's petrol engine with a weight of 130 lbs and an output of 1.5 hp. Outboard motors did not make their appearance until many decades later (see Chapter 6).

The patent description of Anastasia Baumann of

Turbinia, *owned by Sir Charles Parsons, was the first steam-turbine yacht. At Spithead in Britain in 1897 it reached a speed of 35 knots and left all the larger boats standing. She was 103 ft long and only 9 ft on the beam, i.e. a slim pencil with a length-beam ratio of 12:1. Her engine, with an output of 2000 hp, weighed 22 tons including boiler, shaft and propeller. This was half the ship's total weight, which was 44 tons including water and fuel. There was little room left for the crew.*

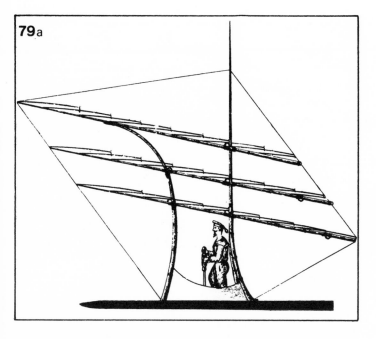

Munich, Germany, dated 26 August 1899, shows how fantastically unrealistic some of the efforts were to give lift to a hull and thereby make it reach higher speeds under engine power. This good lady, without taking into account the additional air resistance, makes the following suggestion: 'The purpose of the present

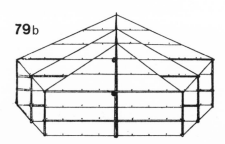

invention is to give lift to water-borne vessels driven by propellers. The ship is fitted with masts or supports, which can be forked at the lower ends to make them rest securely on board. On these masts there are attached light frames covered with strips of sailcloth. These are arranged in tiers that slope upwards towards the forward end of the boat.'

One should not be too hard on Anastasia Baumann but rather blame the German Imperial Patent Office for patenting such nonsense (Figs 79a and 79b) — in return for a sizable fee, of course. Money will buy anything, and this applied in the Kaiser's day as it does now.

The following designs are already of unmistakable planing hulls, especially when compared to the then prevalent types of hull: The narrow, deep 'planks on edge', the over-bred, fast displacement hulls, the Navy's ships of the line. What we notice first about the craft designed by the Frenchman Count Charles de Lambert of Versailles (Fig. 80) is the flat, boarded bottom without a keel and with the propeller shaft passing straight through without any deadwood whatever. But the boat does not plane on this bottom but rather on a series of hollow, prism-shaped appendages fitted to the underside on springs.

What we have here is, in fact, a multi-stepped bottom with steps angled at 2° to 6° and interrupted by gaps rather than being continuous. The purpose of the springs is to enable the steps to alter their position

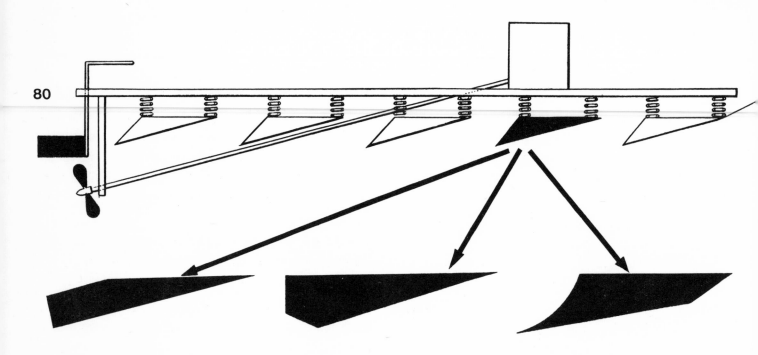

slightly in relation to the bottom and act as shock-absorbers. It is, no doubt, possible that at a certain speed hydrodynamic lift is produced and the boat rests on the underside of the steps alone, and no doubt this reduces friction due to the reduced wetted surface, but the gaps between the steps and their suspension on springs is hardly likely to promote planing qualities, even though the inventor claims to have determined the gaps strictly according to the maximum speed. But the basic idea behind this design must have given future generations food for thought.

The patent description by Marie Gabriel dated 7 February 1906 reflects the current opinion on fast motorboats: 'In fast moving motorboats the propeller shaft is frequently angled downwards to produce an upward-directed propeller thrust, which tends to lift the boat out of the water, thereby reducing its displacement and increasing its speed. For the same purpose inclined planing surfaces are used, and the propeller is enclosed in a tube open at either end in order to concentrate the propeller thrust backwards.'

The 'propeller shaft angled downwards' was, no doubt, necessitated by an inboard engine and hardly produced an 'upward-directed propeller thrust', because the effect of the propeller gets less as the angle between the shaft and the waterline increases. The 'inclined planing surfaces' have just been discussed, and the effectiveness under certain conditions of the 'propeller enclosed in a tube open at either end' has been confirmed by the so-called 'Kort-Jet'. But to 'surround the angled propeller shaft with an equally angled tube the walls of which will act as planing surface' (Fig. 81) is rather too much of a good thing. For, quite apart from the increased form resistance of this additional body below the waterline, the additional frictional resistance of the increased wetted surface would be considerable and cancel out any possible increase in speed.

A remarkable design was patented in 1907 by Axel Holmström of Paris. It was a 'water-borne craft resting on floating runners' (Figs 82—85). It is, in a way, the forerunner to our Hovercraft, incorporating many principles which Cockerell had patented fifty years later. It even has an air-screw to provide alternative propulsion to the water propeller, something which is both possible and necessary in this type of amphibious craft. Perhaps the air-screw also serves as ventilator which, as it is turned by the wind created by the vessel's movement, produces the 'gas, air or the like' which is needed for the functioning of the vessel. Holmström's patent specification makes no mention of how else it is to be produced or whether, perhaps, it is carried on board in bottles.

What we have here is really a motor catamaran (Fig.

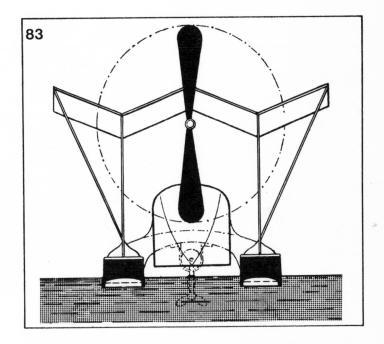

83) the underside of whose hulls is concave (Fig. 84). When the vessel is in motion, this concavity is filled with some gas or other to reduce friction (Fig. 85).

Engine and steering are in the middle between the two parallel hulls, which are hollow and buoyant. Their bottom is curved upwards, i.e. concave, and the sides are extended downwards to prevent the gas escaping. At the bow the bottom of each hull rises up above the surface of the water (Fig. 85) and is fitted with what we now call an 'apron' in Hovercraft. This apron is made of rubber, cloth or some other flexible material. (The working principle of Hovercraft, which until recently was highly controversial, did not become

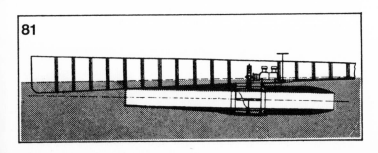

Fig. 82   Craft with skid-like twin hulls by Axel Holmström, Paris, 1907 (side view).

Fig. 84   Craft with skid-like twin hulls by Axel Holmström, Paris, 1907 (section of hull on air cushion).
Fig. 85   Craft with skid-like twin hulls by Axel Holmström, Paris, 1907 (passage of air under the hull).

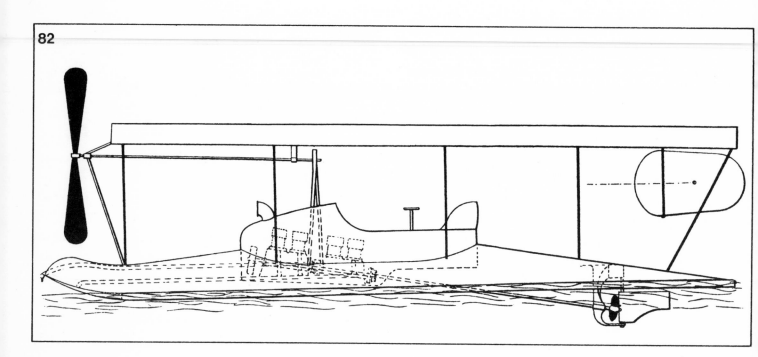

82

financially viable until the perfection of suitable synthetic materials, from which the apron could be made light, flexible and impervious to air.)

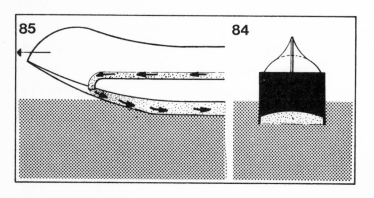

85   **84**

The gas ducts leading forward from the engine emerge behind the apron in the concavity of the bottom, and since their openings are slightly compressed by the resistance of the water when the boat is in motion, the speed of the emerging gas is thereby accelerated, 'which enhances the planing qualities of the hulls'.

This then is the principle of the perfect planing hull, in which the frictional resistance of the water is reduced to a minimum. In those days it was merely a futuristic idea, now it has been put into practice.

One year later, in March 1908, William Henry Fauber of Nanterres in France had his 'planing hull with

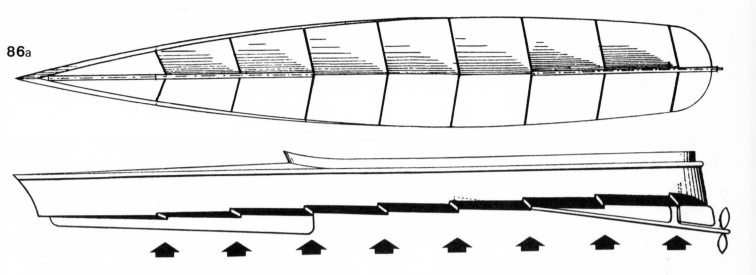

stepped planing surfaces' patented (Fig. 86a). This design was the basis of all later designs of planing hulls. We recognize in it not only the principle of the stepped bottom but also the beginnings of the wide, flat after part of the bottom and the V-section, which the inventor expected would 'favourably affect the stability of the craft'. Thus Fauber's design is also a forerunner of the modern V-bottom and the fast, seaworthy speedboat.

The individual planing surfaces are inclined downwards from bow to stern. Each one is made up of two surfaces forming a V, the tip of the V lying on the keel-line. The chine angle is greater aft than forward, i.e. the bottom is flat forward and V-shaped aft. The individual planing surfaces are either flat or concave to effect the deflection of water which will give the maximum vertical lift. To give the flat forward part of the hull adequate lateral stability a shallow fin is fitted to the bottom from the bow to about half the length of the hull.

A detail, illustrated in Fig. 87b, was patented separate-ly in 1909. By comparison with the original design (Fig. 86b) the stepped planing surfaces are slightly different in that the outer edge of the surface is angled further towards the horizontal than the inner edge.

It is apparent from Fig. 86a that in Fauber's design the characteristics of a planing hull (flat, broad stern) are combined with those of a displacement hull (long and narrow). This shape may have led to higher speeds than those attainable with conventional displacement hulls, but at some point the stern will drop and no further increase in speed is possible. It was well known in 1910 that this had to be avoided, and remedies had been suggested. Commenting on his 'device for maintaining the correct trim of motorboats' invented in February 1912 Wilhelm Struck of Berlin writes: 'To ensure the correct trim of planing hulls the bottom is provided with panels which lift the boat out of the water. Furthermore, rotating blades have been fitted at the stern or at the sides. This arrangement has not proved satisfactory. In the present invention (Figs 88a and 88b) the problem of keeping the boat correctly

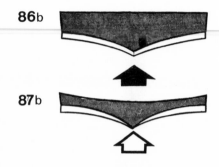

86b

87b

trimmed at high speeds is solved by rigidly connecting to it a second buoyant body.'

The argument is strikingly logical: 'Let us consider the boat in its entire length as a plank which behaves like a

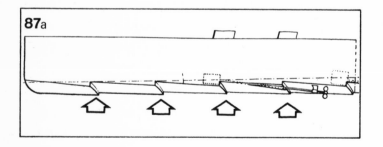

87a

two-armed lever. At high speeds it is lifted up in front by the resistance of the water and pushed under the water by the stern by the suction of the propeller (Fig. 88a). This effect can be counteracted by another boat attached rigidly to the stern of the first boat. This, by its own buoyant lift, produces a turning moment in the opposite direction' (Fig. 88b). The inventor argues that as the first boat is lifted up by the resistance of the water at high speeds the second boat restores the correct longitudinal trim. The first boat (towing another displacement hull of equal weight!) is supposed to rise higher and higher in the water until it is planing! There is a second advantage to this arrangement: it results in a boat of twice the length and displacement, which goes faster than the one boat would. (This may well be possible, because the two boats linked so closely could, hydrodynamically, be considered one body. With the waterline length thus doubled the speed increase, providing there is adequate engine power, could be considerable.)

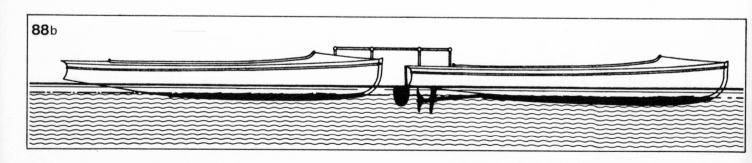

88b

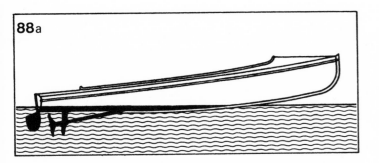

88a

A fantastic idea came from Curt Pinkert of Dresden, Germany in 1920 with his 'friction-reducing planing surfaces' (Fig. 89). This, in his own words, is how he imagined that the performance of planing hulls, even stepped ones, could be improved: 'We know of planing hulls in which part of the bottom is flat and at an angle to the direction of movement. At high speed this produces dynamic lift, which raises the vessel out of the water and thereby removes resistance due to displacement almost completely. Normal ship hulls have experimentally been fitted with rollers and mov-ing belts in the bottom or at the sides of the vessel, but they have not proved successful because they increased the form resistance considerably whilst reducing the frictional resistance only minimally. The point of my invention is to fit a planing hull with continuous belts travelling over rollers, and it is on these that the boat rests in the water. They make it easier for the boat to rise out of the water, because they reduce friction between the water and the relatively large hull area. High speeds become possible, since the friction set up in the bearings of the belt rollers is less than the reduction of friction on the planing surfaces. Thus the only friction to be overcome is air friction along the entire exposed surface of the vessel, while the vastly more important water friction is largely removed and a correspondingly large amount of engine power saved. A useful variation is possible by arranging the belts in steps one behind the other, which ensures particularly good longitudinal stability.' The inventor did not even begin to appreciate how much resistance his belts would set up and how much energy they would use!

In the patent register of 1921 we come across a 'flexibly suspended steering rudder for planing boats' by the Société des Bateaux Glisseurs de Lambert at Nanterres in France (Fig. 90). Since the rudder in a planing boat is particularly at risk, this invention ensures that it gives way if it hits an obstacle. The rudder shaft is fitted with a cylindrical spring which enables it to travel up in the rudder trunk.

Fig. 89 Planing hull on belt rollers by Curt Pinkert, Dresden, Germany, 1920.

Fig. 90 Steering rudder on spring for planing boats patented by the Société des Bateaux Glisseurs, Nanterres, France, 1921.

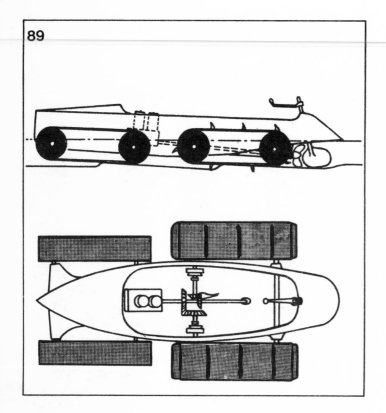

89

A planing vessel on rotating, hollow bodies with a convex surface was thought up in 1925 by Hans Bechem of Uerdingen in Germany (Fig. 92). When at rest the bottom of the vessel sits on the water. As soon as the engine is started and the rotors set in motion, the vessel lifts up so that only the rotors rest on the surface of the water. 'The faster the rotation speed, the greater the lift.'

Hermann Hillmann, in his invention of 1925 (Figs 93 and 94), aims at exploiting the drop shape. 'But in the case of motorboats the absolute drop shape, which would offer the minimum resistance, cannot be used without adaptation, because such a boat, due to its

The remarkable feature about the design by the Berlin engineer Wesnigk (Fig. 91) is not so much the 'main planing surface' under the forward part of the hull (an early form of hydrofoil with which I do not want to deal at this point) but the springy tail fin at the stern. Being forked and capable of being twisted, it is used to bank the vessel and thereby steer it.

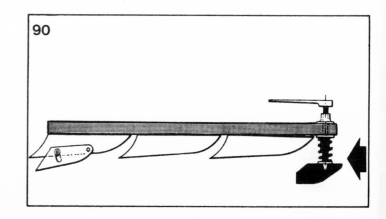

90

Fig. 91 Planing hull patented by Mr Wesnigk, Berlin, Germany, 1920.

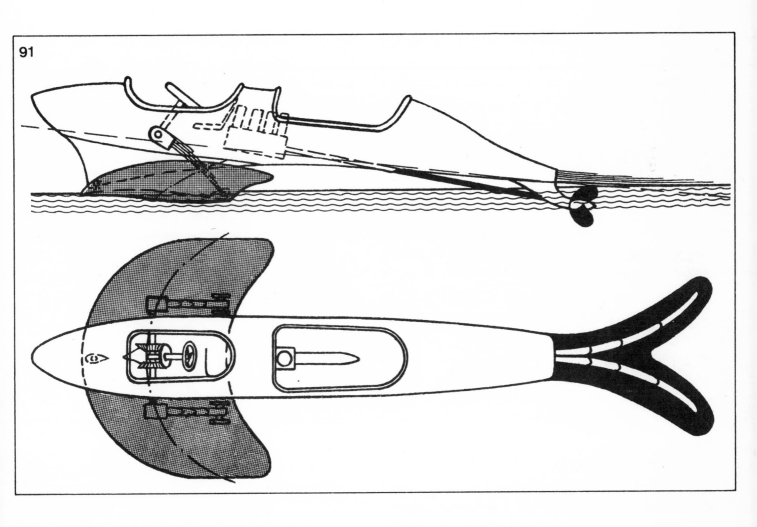

pointed stern, would not lie in the water as it should.' Thus Hillmann combines two drop-shaped hulls in such a way that they form one single drop in the forward part, whereas the two pointed sterns diverge. The inventor points out that the wetted surface is reduced to a minimum and that his design is in line with current enlightened efforts to dispense with all those parts on a planing hull which would unnecessarily increase the wetted surface once the boat reaches a certain speed. Looking at the half-section (Fig. 94)

Fig. 92 Planing hull with rotors by Hans Bechem, Uerdingen, Germany, 1925.

Fig. 93 Drop-shaped planing hull by Hermann Hillmann, 1925 (side view and plan view).

Fig. 94 Drop-shaped planing hull by Hermann Hillmann, 1925 (section).

there can be no doubt that the hull has a bottom shape favourable to planing.

The following device (Fig. 95) patented by Johannes Plum of Washington, USA in 1926, which is a small tab at the stern pivoting round a vertical axis, is actually a forerunner of our modern trim tabs. We have here a stepped hull, under which the water can flow uninterruptedly from the after edge of the forward step to the stern, which rests on a fin-shaped tab. This can be pivoted horizontally through 45° on each side and thus efficiently support the stern at all speeds, on all courses and also when turning in a circle.

A bow-wave deflector rather like a very broad rubbing strake from the bow to midships and extending from approximately half the freeboard height downwards to just above the waterline (Figs 96 and 97) was patented in 1926 by the German firm of Siemens-Schuckert AG in Berlin. This might be called a forerunner of the

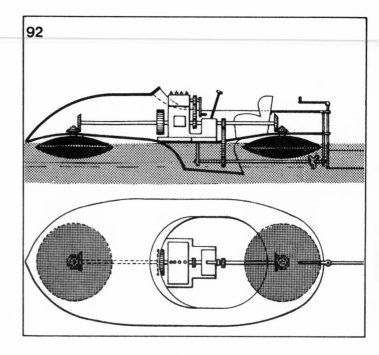

92

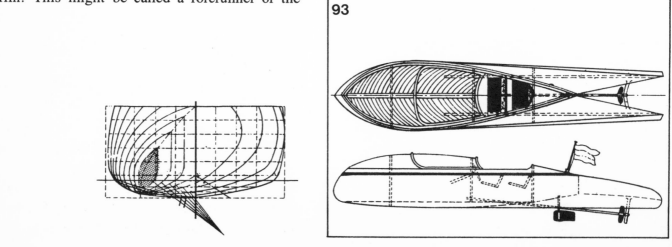

93

94

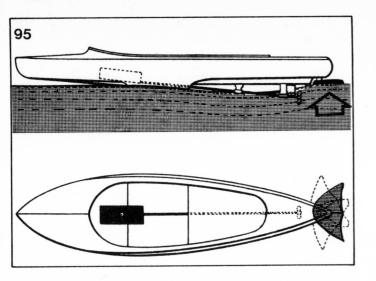

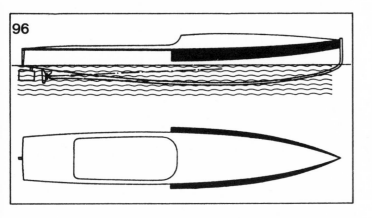

Fig. 95 Stepped planing hull with stern support by Johannes Plum, Washington, USA, 1926.

Fig. 96 Patented wave deflectors for improving the planing qualities of a hull. By Siemens-Schuckert AG, Berlin, 1926 (side view and plan view).

Fig. 97 Patented wave-deflectors for improving the planing qualities of a hull. By Siemens-Schuckert AG, Berlin, 1926 (detail).

Fig. 98 Patented stern for planing hull by Schiffswerft Rosslau, East Germany, 1962.

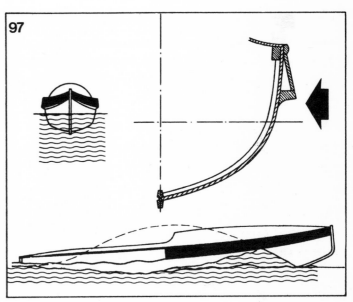

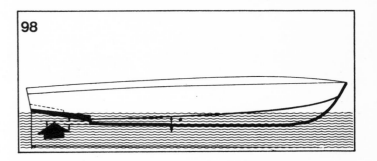

spray strakes as used on the Chrysler boats in 1968 (Fig. 143). The aim of the wave deflectors is to harness the dynamic force of the bow wave into stabilizing the boat and at the same time reduce friction to a minimum, thus increasing the speed of the boat considerably. To avoid unnecessary speed loss through friction, the wave deflector was made only just wide enough to deflect the bow wave, 1/12 to 1/15 of the boat's beam was considered to be the ideal width. Its lower edge had to be 10 inches above the water at its lowest point.

The last of our patented designs for improving the planing qualities of hulls came in 1962 from the East German shipyard of Rosslau (Fig. 98). It concerns a special hull shape at the stern through which wave resistance is reduced, behaviour in a seaway improved and speed increased. The bottom has a step at approximately 20 per cent of the boat's length from the stern, and the bottom panel aft of the step can be adjusted to the angle most favourable at any particular speed.

5 In Search of an Outboard Motor

Figs. 99a and 99b (over) Outboard drive by R. M. Fryer, Washington, USA, 1897.

Fascinating as it may have been to drive a water-borne vessel by a fast rotating screw (only later called 'propeller') under the stern, this had one disadvantage compared to the previously used slow paddlewheel mounted on the side of the hull: the drive shaft had to pass through the hull *under* water and in the very spot where a displacement hull (which was the only type built then) should be as pointed as possible to offer the least resistance. The hole through which the shaft passed had to be watertight and well packed. This posed problems especially in small boats where the stern post in that area had to be especially thick and if possible grown in one piece. There was, therefore, no shortage of efforts to overcome these drawbacks by developing an outboard drive, either by power trans-mission *above* the water from an inboard motor to a separate outboard drive, or by mounting the entire drive unit including the motor on the *outside* of the hull.

These efforts were spurred on by yet another disadvantage inherent in screw propulsion: The propeller could easily be damaged by accidentally touching bottom or striking drifting objects, or it could be put out of action by entangled water plants and seagrass. If a paddlewheel got damaged under water the wheel was simply turned until the damaged part was above the water, where it could easily be put right. A damaged screw was not so easy to repair. The boat had to be beached, a larger vessel hauled out of the water or put into dry-dock.

It is difficult to separate precisely the early history of the inboard/outboard drive (or Z-drive) and that of the actual outboard motor. Since, however, common beginnings evolved into two distinctly different types of propulsion, we must try to classify them apart from the start.

The idea of mounting the propeller unit on the side of the hull like a paddlewheel first occurred to R.M. Fryer of Washington, USA in 1897 (Figs 99a and 99b). His outboard drive was streamlined like a torpedo, but the torpedo only contained harmless cogwheels and differentials which were necessary to transmit the power at right angles. His idea remained pure theory, however.

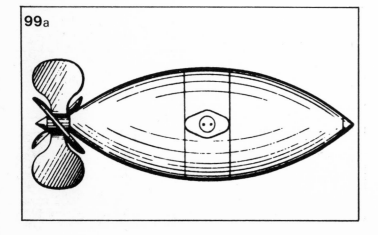

99a

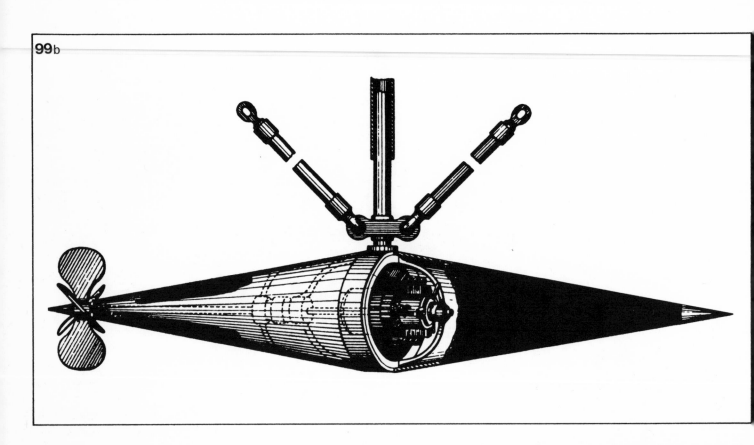

99b

The inboard/outboard drive patented by the French Société des Propulseurs Universel Avomobile of Neuilly in 1899 strikes us as surprisingly modern by comparison (Fig. 100). It already has all the typical features of a modern Z-drive, and it was series-built in what in those days were large numbers. Why the 1.75 hp motor for petrol or alcohol, weighing approximately 140 lbs and built mainly of aluminium, should have fallen into oblivion is hard to understand.

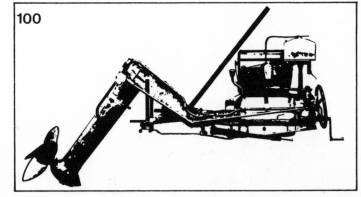

100

Fig. 101   Outboard   drive   by   Cudell   &   Co.,   Berlin,
Germany, 1904.

Another firm engaged in developing an outboard drive
was the German firm of Cudell & Co of Berlin in 1904
(Fig. 101). They simply mounted the whole drive unit
on the transom, with the rigidly connected propeller
shaft passing straight down at an angle. The design
illustrates the limitations of this type of drive, which
eventually led to the separate development of in-
board/outboard and pure outboard drive: with the shaft
angled at 45° the propeller is inefficient.

This may also be the reason why the 'Lautonautile'
illustrated in Fig. 100 ceased to be built. The Cudell-
drive, incidentally, weighed 88 lbs, and the engine
output was 2 hp. The whole thing was intended
primarily for military use. It was revived, almost

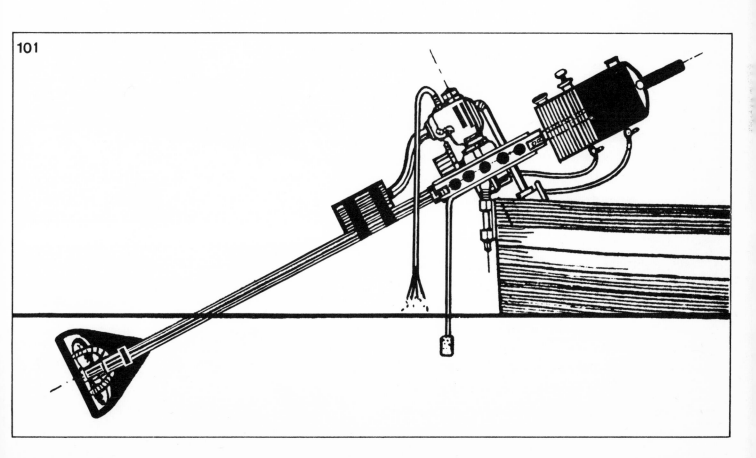

101

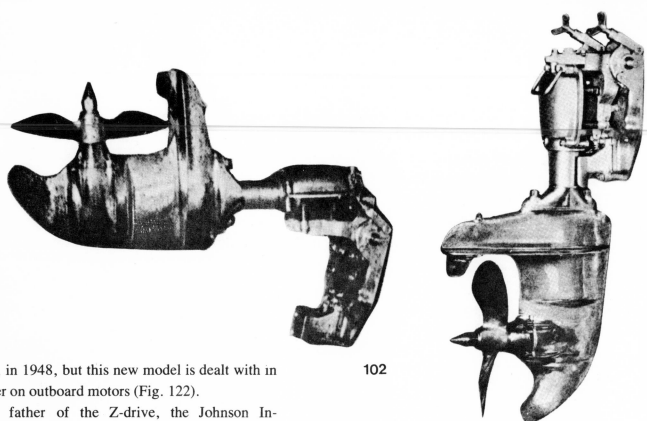

102

unaltered, in 1948, but this new model is dealt with in the chapter on outboard motors (Fig. 122).

The true father of the Z-drive, the Johnson Inboard/Outboard Drive developed in 1930, unfortunately fell into neglect during the world economic crisis (Fig. 102). Here again is a design which was way ahead of its time and of popular demand. Some of its features, like the underwater shape, cavitation plate, exhaust system and tilting shaft, were hardly different from the Z-drives of 1960.

In 1951 Josef Wutzer of Munich had a screw drive patented in which the drive motor was connected by a flexible shaft with the outboard drive, which was permanently bolted to the hull but could be moved up and down (Figs 103 and 104). As an alternative the motor could be mounted directly on the vertical shaft. The hinged brackets enable the propeller to be raised if

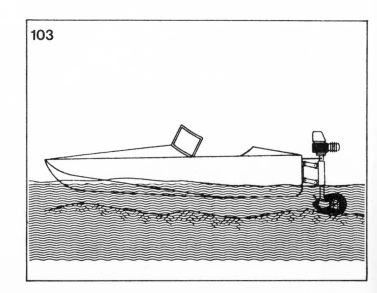

103

Fig. 104 Wutzer's patent either as inboard engine with flexible shaft to the outboard drive or, alternatively, as rigid outboard motor.

Fig. 105 Outboard drive by Murray & Tregurtha Inc, USA, 1942.

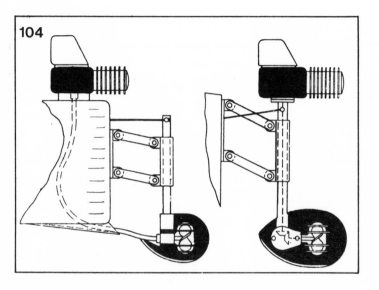

104

105

it accidentally touches ground. The propeller itself is encased in a rudder-shaped blade so that it can also be used for steering.

The patented design by Murray & Tregurtha Inc. of Quincy, USA (Figs 105 and 106) clearly illustrates the problems which had to be overcome on the way to our modern Z-drive. The transmission of power from the horizontal engine shaft to the upper end of the vertical drive shaft to the lower end of which is connected the propeller shaft, once again at right angles, produces a very strong turning moment. This seeks to twist the unit round its vertical axis and puts considerable strain on it, especially on the steering mechanism. The turning moment aids steering in one direction but opposes it in the other. In Murray & Tregurtha's

model, which is still produced today, the engine transmission is led to one side of the drive shaft casing in order to neutralize the turning moment. Modern Z-drives deal with this problem by having the shaft from the engine to the outboard drive positioned lower and led outboard immediately above or below the water surface (Figs 107 to 109).

Murray & Tregurtha's drive is unusual in a number of other respects: the outboard drive can be tilted hydraulically, and the transmission from engine shaft to propeller shaft is by bevel-wheels.

The first German Z-drive came from Friedrich Korner of Hanau, but the inventor, unfortunately, did not have

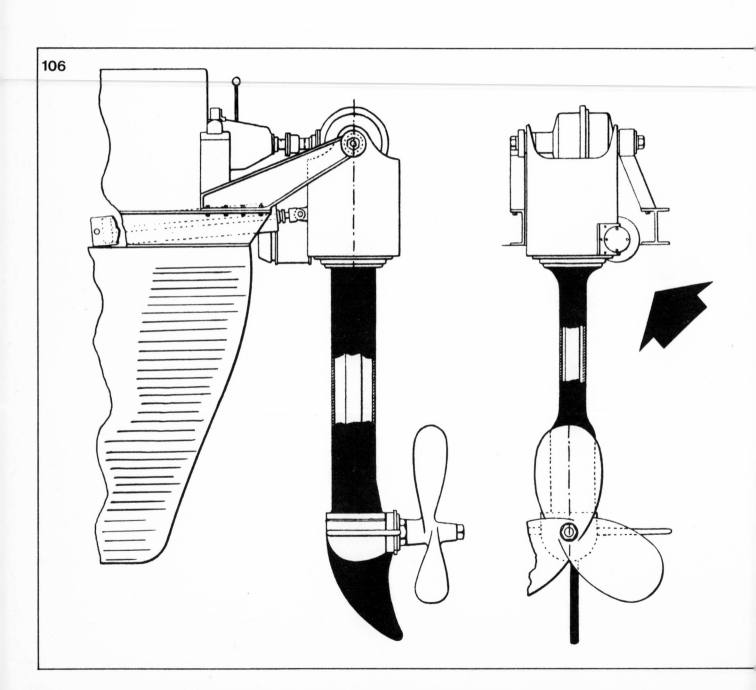

106

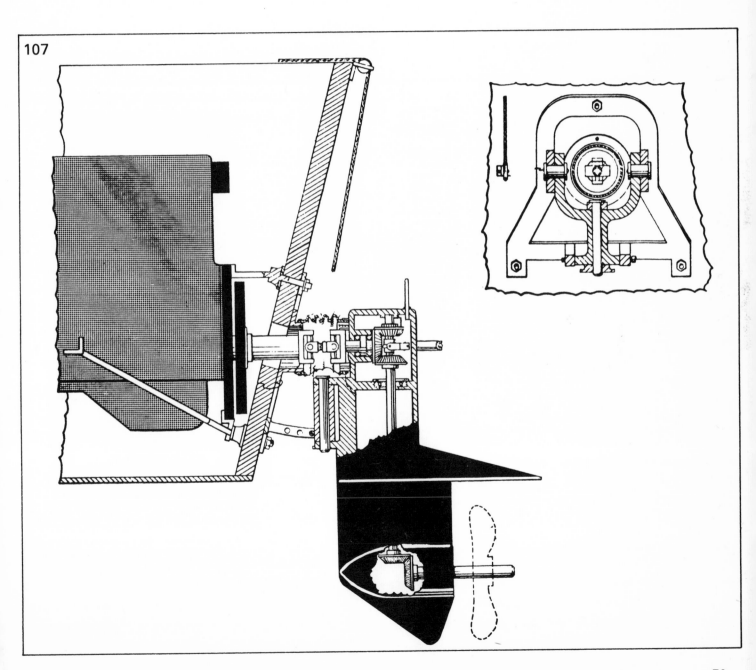

Fig. 107 The patent by James R. Wynne, USA, illustrates the concept of the modern Z-drive (1958).

107

Fig. 108   Z-drive with chain transmission and feathering propeller by Willy Dost, Hildesheim in Germany, 1956.

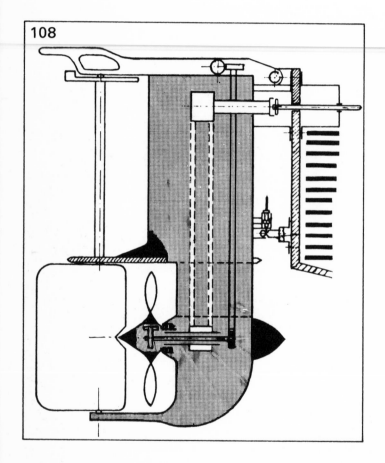

and cone wheels but single or multiple drive chains (Fig. 108). It has a feathering propeller and can be tilted up. Although it claimed to offer low-noise operation and easier lubrication it never became popular.

The American James R. Wynne, on the other hand, who had worked for some time at the Kiekhaefer Research Centre on Lake X in Florida, designed a successful modern Z-drive in 1958 (Fig. 108). In the same year, when he stayed with Ole Botved in Denmark to prepare for his Atlantic crossing in a motor cruiser, he sold his idea to Volvo Penta in Gothenburg, Sweden, who had it patented (Fig. 109). In 1959 the first model of the famous Volvo-Penta-Aquamatic Z-drive, of which 90,000 units were built in 1970, was on show at the Chicago Boat Show.

The principal improvement of the Volvo-Penta Aquamatic drive over previous Z-drives, in which the outboard-drive was rigidly connected with the motor, is its special transom plate incorporating universal coupling, which prevents vibration from the motor and propeller from being transmitted to the hull. At the same time the flexible sleeve enclosing the coupling serves as effective seal for the opening in the transom.

The Z-drive is nowadays the most popular means of propulsion for speedboats, because it can be made to tilt up automatically when striking underwater obstacles, thus protecting the propeller from damage. It

it patented. It was marketed in limited numbers under the name of 'Hai-Drive' in the late fifties.

The Z-drive which Willy Dost of Hildesheim in Germany had patented in 1956 does not use rigid shafts

Fig. 109   The patented Volvo-Penta Aquamatic Z-drive (1959).

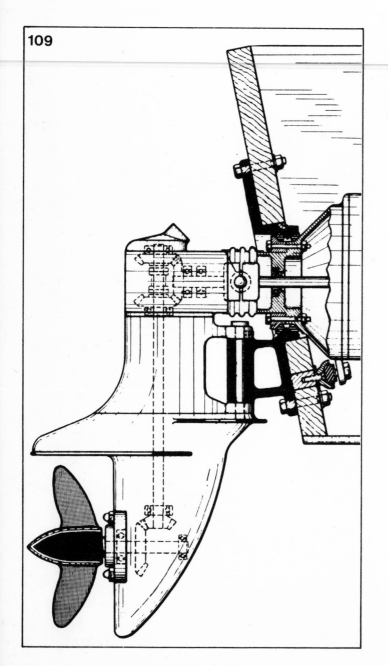

109

can also be tilted up when the boat is on the mooring or when the propeller needs replacing. The fact that it pierces the hull above or very little below the waterline is a further advantage.

6 Outboard Motors Have Their Own History

Fig. 110 *Electric outboard motor by Frank G. Curtis, New York, 1892.*
Fig. 111 *Electric outboard motor by W. Griscom, Philadelphia, USA, 1882.*

110

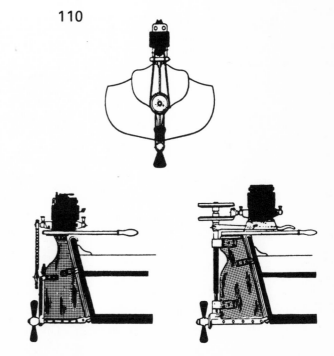

We have already touched on the reasons for the development of the outboard motor. If we consider that at the turn of the century a 1 hp motor still weighed as much as 90 lbs we realize that the ingenuity of inventors was curbed by technical progress. An outboard motor had to be light yet efficient. This ruled out the internal combustion engine and limited the choice of propulsion power at the outset of outboard history to electricity and steam.

The great-grandfather of our modern outboard motor is an electric outboard motor developed by the Frenchman Gustave Trouvé, which was exhibited at the Paris International Exhibition of 1881 (Fig. 112). Its propeller turns in a window cut out of the large rudder blade. The electric motor is simply screwed on to a wooden shelf over the rudder, and power transmission to the propeller is by a chain drive. The wires leading from the motor forward to the batteries also serve as steering wires. According to reports the boat driven by this first outboard motor reached a speed of 3 knots with four people on board.

The electric outboard motor patented in 1882 by W. Griscom of Philadalphia USA (Fig. 111), in which we particularly notice the discrepancy in size between motor, flywheel and propeller, remained theory. The following design by Frank G. Curtis of New York (1892) seems rather more practical by comparison (Fig. 110). He simply attaches the propeller to the after edge of the rudder blade. Power transmission from the

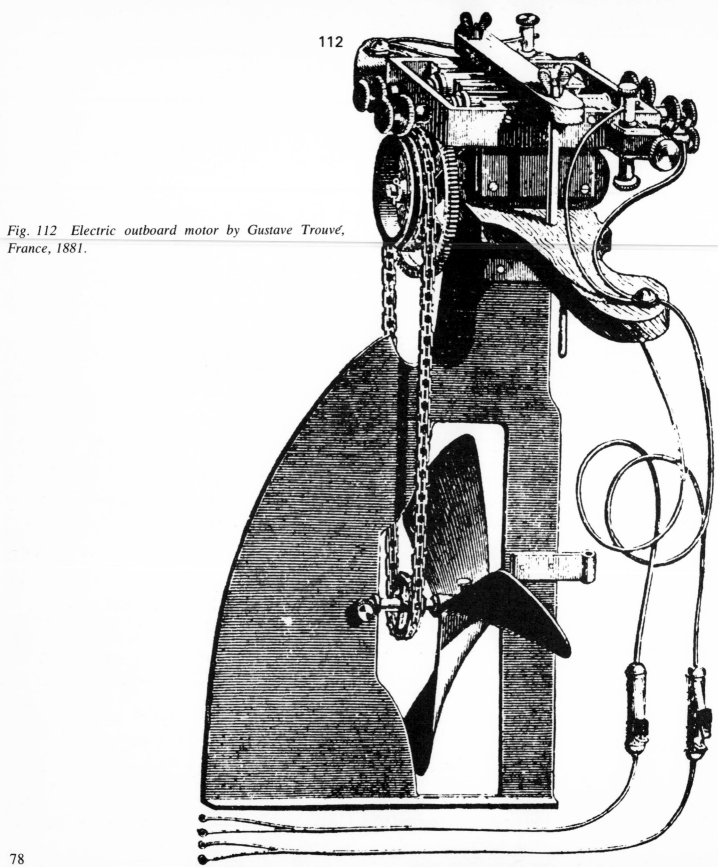

112

Fig. 112   Electric outboard motor by Gustave Trouvé, France, 1881.

Fig. 113 Electric outboard motor by the Englishman E. du Boulay, 1895.

Fig. 114 Outboard with steam engine by S. Emerson Harthan, USA, 1887.

Fig. 115 Outboard combustion engine by American Motors Company, New York, 1896.

Fig. 116 Outboard combustion engine with seawater cooling and feathering propeller by Albert T. Otto, 1900.

electric motor above the rudder blade to the propeller is once again by chain drive, or rather by two chain drives with a set of gears between them. As with more recent outboard motors steering is by tiller, with the 'throttle' right next to it. The whole drive and steering unit, which is hung on the stern by gudgeons and pintles, can 'easily and quickly be removed from the boat and attached to another boat', to use the inventor's own words.

An Englishman, E. du Boulay, in his electric outboard motor of 1895 (Fig. 113), uses a belt drive instead of a

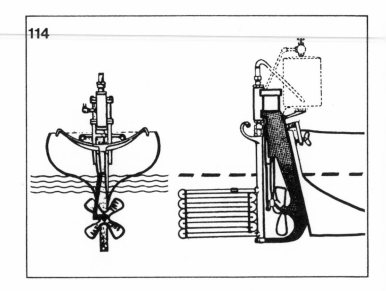

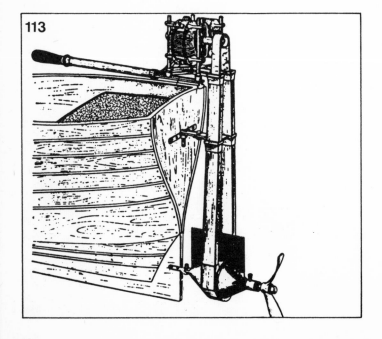

chain drive, and the bulb-shaped propeller unit with the small rudder already points the way to the modern outboard shape.

All these electric units had one drawback, however: the motor was too heavy. One accumulator consisting of 6 batteries each of 12 plates 6 in square and weighing 26 lbs each had a weight of approximately 180 lbs including the wooden carrying box and took up a space on board of over 3 sq. ft. This made it impossible to carry much else on board.

S. Emerson Harthan of Massachusetts, USA, in 1887 tried to drive an outboard motor with steam (Fig. 114). The piston rod was coupled directly to the propeller

115

shaft, and the rudder was made up of a system of pipes, in which the steam was condensed back into water for re-use. It appears, however, that the system was never tried and the unit never built, because the inventor says nothing about the source of energy which is to drive the steam engine on top of the outboard motor.

The first practical attempt to use an internal combustion engine for driving an outboard propeller was made in 1896 by the American Motors Company of New York (Fig. 115), who used an already proven petrol motor. Their unit already had a vertical crank shaft and drive shaft, cone-wheel gears and a horizontal propeller shaft, which is usual in most outboard motors today. The four-stroke one-cylinder engine with as

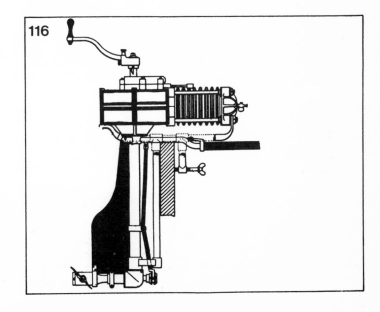

116

Fig. 117   First series-produced outboard combustion engine by Cameron B. Waterman, 1906.

Fig. 118   Adjustable drive unit in stern well by Adolf Loffler, Cologne, Germany, 1913.

Fig. 119   Water tractor by Hans Bergmann, Berlin, 1927.

Fig. 120   Water tractor by Hans Bergmann, Berlin, 1927. Detail of drive aggregate with tank, cooling system, exhaust etc.

Fig. 121   Jet-outboard by H. J. McCollum, Chicago, USA, 1946.

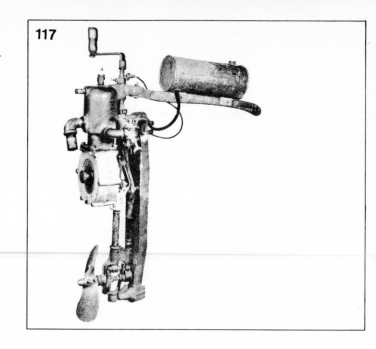

much as 80 mm (3 1/8 in) bore and 100 mm (4 in) stroke, doing 400 to 600 rpm, developed 1 hp. Air cooling was by a coil of thick wire round the outside of the cylinder casting, rather like the fins enclosing our modern air-cooled cylinders. Ignition was by a dry cell with an induction coil.

The first patented outboard combustion-engine, in 1900, was that by Albert T. Otto (Fig. 116), which had a cooling system by seawater and a feathering propeller. This was obviously too ambitious for its time, for it was never built in series.

Cameron B. Waterman, on the other hand, who as law student at Yale University in the United States of America in 1903 had come in touch with a few patents, was well on the road to success when he decided to build engines for motor vehicles and outboard motors. He founded a factory in Detroit and began by building twenty-five portable engines in 1906 (Fig. 117), followed in 1907 by 3,000 series-built engines.

At first Waterman used a Curtis motor-cycle engine to drive a propeller with a chain drive. The 1907 series were water-cooled one-cylinder motors with a flywheel enclosed in the crankcase. They were perfected as far as the Model C-14 built in 1914, which has a flywheel magneto.

In 1913 Adolf Löffler of Cologne, Germany, tried to solve the outboard-drive problem in a different way (Fig. 118): he put the motor and everything that went with it into a floating tank, which fitted into a well in the stern. It could be raised and lowered so that the propeller could always be set at the same height in

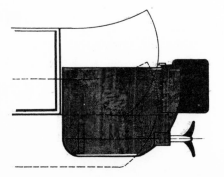
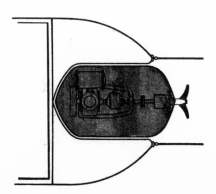

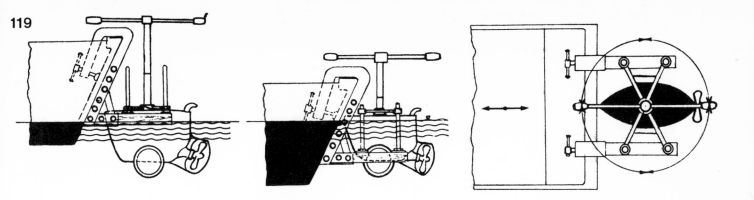

119

relation to the surface of the water, no matter how high or low the boat was in the water. This 'floating outboard unit' was meant to be used primarily on larger boats and ships and be exchanged between vessels of the same type.

Hans Bergmann of Berlin must have been guided by similar ideas when he had his 'water tractor' patented in 1927 (Figs 119 and 120). In his design, too, the whole drive unit including motor, fuel tank and propeller is housed in a separate, floating container which can be attached not only to the stern but also to the bow and which can be adapted to fit transoms of different heights. It can be turned through 360°, and to top it all it is fitted with wheels for easy transport to and from the boat.

The first jet outboard motor, patented in 1946, was designed by H.J. McCollum of Chicago, USA (Fig. 121). The fuel is burnt in a combustion chamber in a series of energy bursts which are controlled by a reed valve at the air inlet. The exhaust gases leave through a

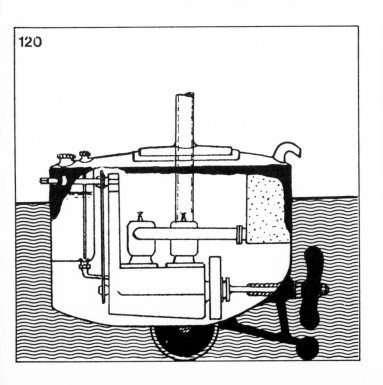

120

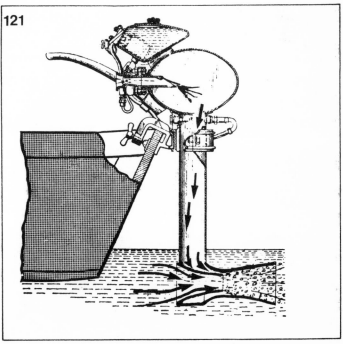

121

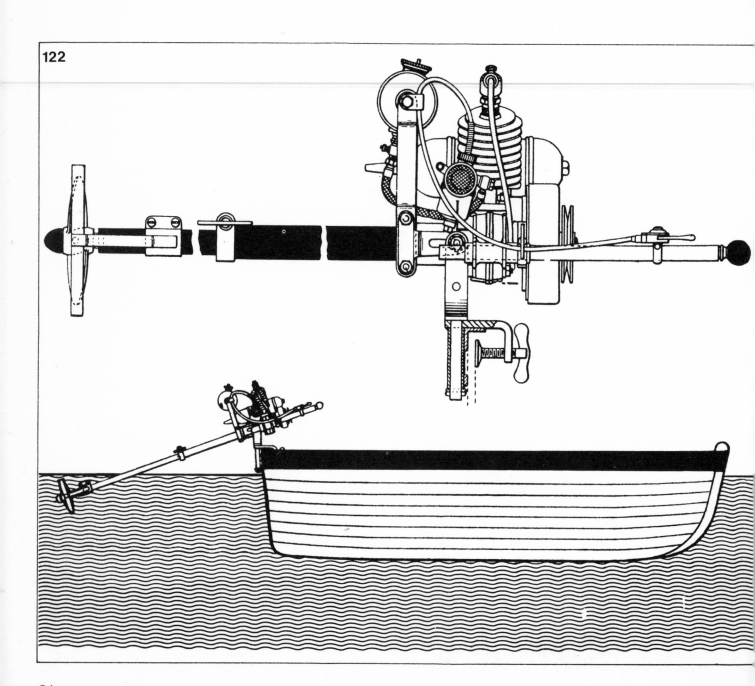

Fig. 122   Portable drive unit clamped to the transom by
John Geoffrey Pugh, Birmingham, England, 1948.
Fig. 123   Pivoting outboard which can be turned through
360° by Leopold Jantschke, Stuttgart, Germany, 1951.

122

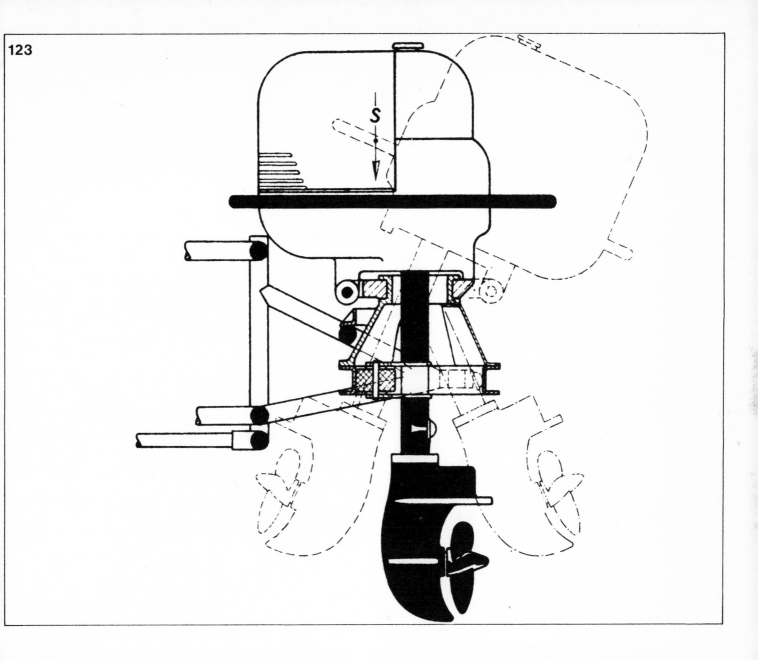

ring-shaped valve round the water inlet just under the surface of the water. When the kinetic energy of the exhaust gases have been passed to the water at the point where the valve narrows, the whole mixture, with reduced pressure, is expelled into the open water aft.

Fig. 122 shows how effortlessly a patent can be obtained for an idea even if the basic concept has been patented before some time ago. We have already met with a very similar design in Fig. 100. The outboard motor designed by John Geoffrey Pugh of Birmingham, England in 1948 is detachable and portable. It fits on the transom and is so proportioned that it is always balanced, even when the boat is moving. The propeller is attached to a flexible shaft.

Leopold Jäntschke is the inventor of an outboard unit whose shaft and propeller can be turned through 360°, so that it can drive the boat in all directions (Fig. 123).

Fig. 124   Outboard motor with underwater cylinders by Giorgio Solaroli, Turin, Italy, 1952.

It is hung on the stern by a bracket which is adjustable in height and which allows the motor to be tilted if it should accidentally strike an underwater obstacle, no matter how it is angled to the course.

An outboard motor whose cylinders were under water was invented in 1952 by Giorgio Solaroli of Turin in Italy (Fig. 124). The inventor was of the opinion that conventional outboard motors had the drawback of being very complicated pieces of machinery that had to be assembled in many stages, which led to unnecessarily high production costs. This outboard is carried on a vertical, suspended shaft made in a single casting to include the cylinder head. The shaft head and at least a part of the exhaust system can be made in one casting.

It would seem to me, though, that the main advantage lies in the absence of a vertical drive shaft and the usual gear wheels between it and the horizontal propeller shaft. In this design crank shaft and propeller shaft are one single unit, and the other parts can be dispensed with. On the other hand the resistance of the massive underwater part is considerable, and it might also be difficult to make this motor watertight. As far as is known it has never gone into production.

The English firm of Kenneth & Co. produced an outboard in 1950 in which the propeller is horizontal rather than vertical (Fig. 125). The water is sucked up from below and accelerated as it is expelled aft. Since the engine is directly coupled to the propeller, there is

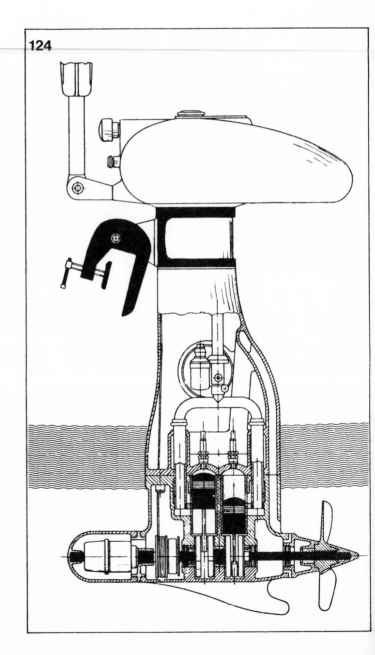

124

Fig. 125 Outboard motor with horizontal propeller by Kenneth & Co., England, 1950.
Fig. 126 Outboard motor in watertight box by Victor Norman Davies, Leigh-on-Sea, England, 1951.

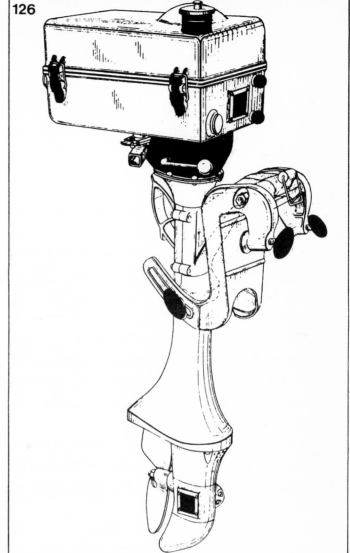

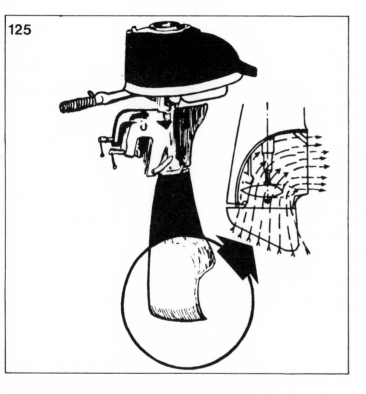

Fig. 125 Outboard motor with horizontal propeller by Kenneth & Co., England, 1950.
Fig. 126 Outboard motor in watertight box by Victor Norman Davies, Leigh-on-Sea, England, 1951.

no need for the usual underwater transmission nor for a reduction gear, and the unit should be mechanically very efficient.

Although there is a lot to be said for this idea, it never became popular. Hydraulically it was obviously not satisfactory. Whilst a normal, vertically arranged propeller has an unrestricted influx of water, this one has to suck the water up before it can accelerate it. The conventional propeller is at its most efficient when working from a standstill, but although this horizontal propeller is permanently working under standstill conditions, the advantages arising from this are likely to be cancelled out by other drawbacks.

The most recent link in the development of outboard motors seems to be the design by Victor Norman Davies of Leigh-on-Sea, Essex, England which was patented in 1951 (Fig. 126). He encloses a conventional outboard in a watertight box to protect it against spray, rain, dirt and mechanical damage. The lid of the box, which rests on a sealing strip and is made fast with clips and hinges, is hollow and serves at the same time as fuel tank.

7 All Kinds of 'New-Fangled' Bottom Shapes

Fig. 127   Tunnelled hull designed by Carl H. Fowler, New York, 1916.

There has never been a shortage of attempts to make the propeller more efficient by changing the shape of the hull bottom. Many special hull sections have been patented, which aim at fulfilling all the hydrodynamic conditions consistent with speed, seaworthiness, stability and other essential qualities. Nearly all the ones dealt with here fall into the period before the widespread use of plastics. Since plastics have made it possible to build hulls in any desired shape it has become increasingly difficult to have every small modification protected by a patent.

Let us begin our survey of bottoms specially designed for greater propeller efficiency with a tunnelled hull by Carl H. Fowler of New York (Fig. 127) which he had patented in 1916. The aim of this design was to prevent the penetration of air into the propeller area, to steady the flow of water from above and to prevent cavitation. Fowler not only raised the bottom to form a tunnel but incorporated a tall water chamber reaching above deck level, from which the cooling water is syphoned to the motor. The motor needs cooling water anyway, and in this way it is supplied with it without any further use of power. But Fowler's hypothesis that the water pressure in which the propeller works is equal to the height of the water in the syphon could not be substantiated.

Another design aimed at increasing the propeller thrust was the tunnel-hull by Gustav Hahn and Gustav Schröder of Berlin patented in 1922. The tunnel

127

Fig. 128   Hull with propeller tunnel by Gustav Hahn and
Gustav Schröder, Berlin, 1922.
Fig. 129   Grooved hull bottom by J. Anderssen, Neckars-
ulm, Germany, 1923.

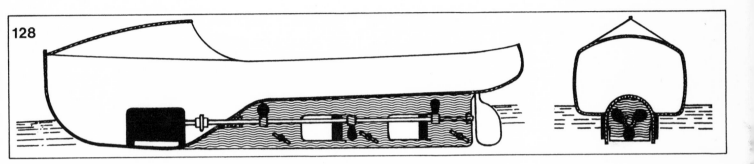

extends over two-thirds of the boat's length from the
stern. In it three single, spaced-out propeller blades
turn on a long shaft. The tunnel walls have openings at
the sides with deflectors at the forward edge, which
direct the water into the tunnel.

J. Anderssen of Neckarsulm in Germany thought up a
hull shape (Fig. 129) in which water flows with
increased pressure along longitudinal channels in the
bottom. Broad channels on either side start immediately behind the bow, get narrower aft and eventually
converge to make a single channel aft of the propeller.
The aim of these channels is not only to accelerate the
water to exert pressure on the tunnel walls and thus
support the stern and lift the boat out of the water.

The possibilities of this design have by no means been
fully appreciated yet as is shown by a comparatively
recent patent by Robert Bruce Stuart of Penn Yan,

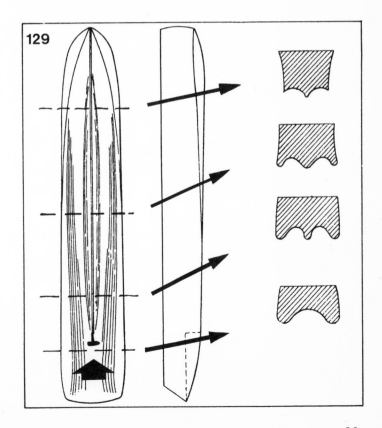

Fig. 130 Planing hull with propeller tunnel by Robert Bruce Stuart, Penn Yan, USA, 1968.

Fig. 131 Propeller tunnel with rigid fin, rudder and splash plate as patented by Robert Bruce Stuart, Penn Yan, USA, 1968 (side view).

Fig. 132 Propeller tunnel with rigid fin, rudder and splash plate as patented by Robert Bruce Stuart, Penn Yan, USA, 1968 (view from below).

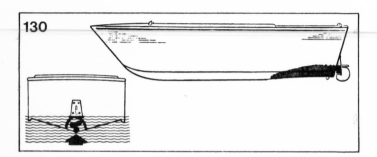

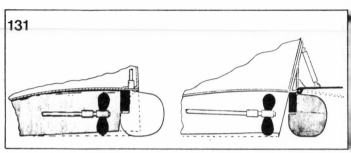

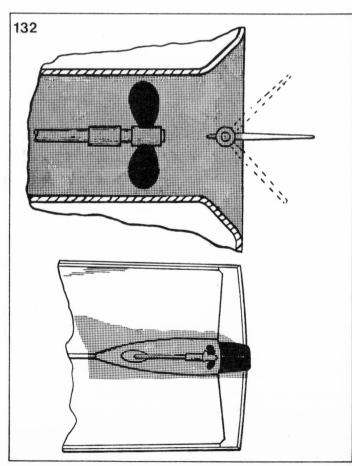

USA (Figs 130—132). In order to improve the steering qualities of a deep-V planing hull, to reduce its draught and utilize the drive power more economically, he proposes a tunnel under the stern which ascends and opens out towards the transom (Fig. 130). The propeller is inside this tunnel and the rudder blade is placed just aft of its opening, with a hinged splash-plate above it (Fig. 131).

At the forward edge of the rudder blade, just aft of the propeller, there is a rigid fin which is to straighten the flow of water from the propeller, while the profiled rudder is to divert it according to the direction in which the boat is steered (Fig. 132). It would appear that tunnel-hulls are still in their infancy.

The development of motor catamarans was initiated in 1914 by William Albert Hickman of South Boston, USA with his 'Sea sled' (Fig. 133). This is a rectangu-

Fig. 133 Sea Sled by William Albert Hickman, South Boston, USA, 1914.

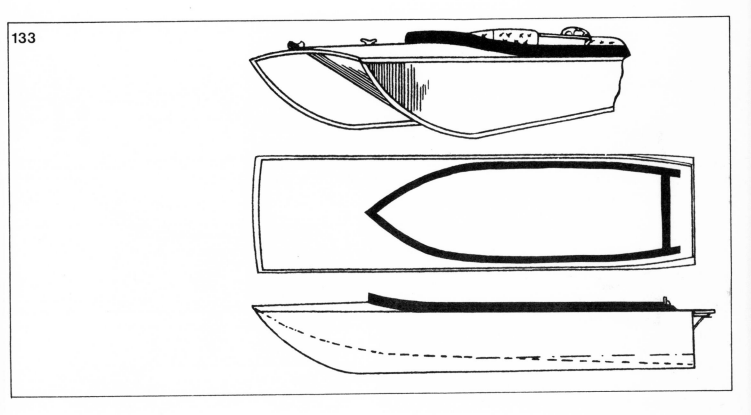

lar hull with vertical sides and an A-section forward, which diminishes towards the stern into a flat run characteristic of planing hulls. 'In this way we get a hull which has proved extremely seaworthy,' the inventor says in his patent specification. 'Spray is not formed along the sides of the hull but in the tunnel between the two hulls. The formation of spray draws a large amount of air into this tunnel, so that the boat more or less skims along on a cloud of foam, and an air cushion is formed, which reduces friction and leads to an increase in the speed of the boat.' Hickman's idea has certainly given a lead to future generations of designers, but the principle was not really fully exploited until comparatively recently, when plywood and plastics became commonly used materials in the construction of fast motorboats.

The 'Motor Scow' designed by Austin Farrar of Ipswich, England, in 1966 is a development of the Hickman Sea Sled design. It is, in fact, an improvement on the Sea Sled which, owing to its V-shape and

Fig. 134   Lines of the Motor Scow designed by Austin Farrar of Ipswich, England, in 1966, which is a development of the Hickman Sea Sled (side elevation, underneath plan and front elevation).

Fig. 135   Wedge-shaped step in the hull designed by Paul Bonnemaison, Vitry-sur-Seine, France, 1922.

134

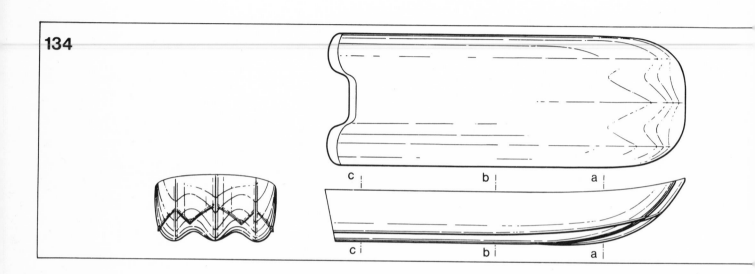

135

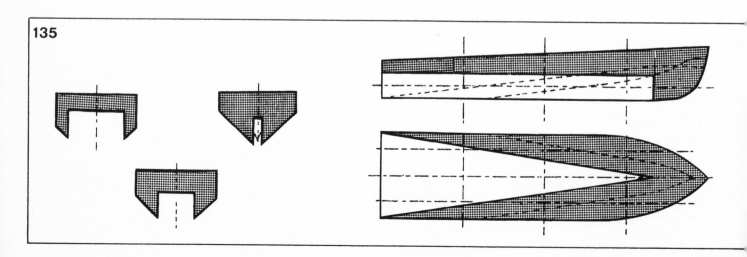

Fig. 136 Combined displacement and planing hull by Pieter van Wienen, Hamburg, Germany, 1925.

conventional wooden construction, showed a tendency to split down the middle.

The Motor Scow, which is built in glass fibre, has in effect three hulls: a central hull and two wing hulls. The central hull breaks up the waves running between the wing hulls and then dies out aft of midships, leaving the wing hulls to run to the stern. All hull surfaces are rounded to reduce the pounding effect of flat surfaces on waves, so that the forward sections are two inverted U's becoming a single inverted U flattening towards the stern.

Waves and spray tend to pass between the hulls, so very little is blown aboard, and the boat gives a drier and smoother ride than a conventional boat because of the air cushion on which it rides. The scow has so far been built as a fast motor launch, but the patented hull form, because of its great stability and seaworthiness, is suitable also for fishing trawlers and ferry boats.

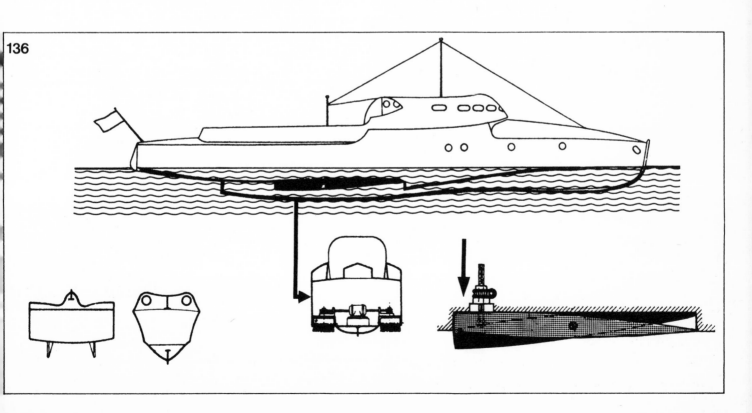

136

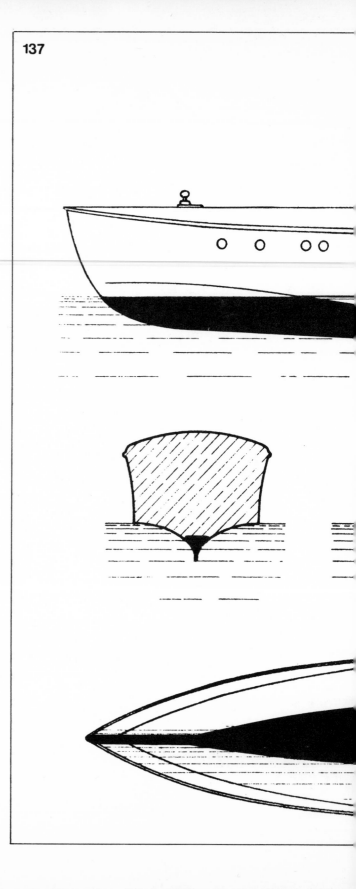

Fig. 137 Displacement hull with transverse step by Pieter van Wienen, Hamburg, 1928.

Another one who wanted to improve the speed and seaworthiness of planing hulls was the Frenchman Paul Bonnemaison from Vitry-sur-Seine in 1922 with his stepped hull (Fig. 135). This has longitudinal steps along the bottom that get narrower aft and between them a tunnel, which becomes correspondingly wider aft. The aim of this design was to ensure an equal distribution of pressure over the whole of the hull (and give larger boats built of the materials then prevalent greater longitudinal rigidity) and also to give the boat fine lines that would reduce buffeting by waves. At high speeds the boat was supposed to lift like a normal planing hull and remain in touch with the water only along a negligible area at the stern. This is the correct Hickman-principle in reverse.

A combination of a displacement hull and a planing hull is what Pieter van Wienen from Hamburg, Germany, designed in 1925 (Fig. 136). Being a yachtsman himself he had experienced how, in bad weather or in a swell, planing hulls can become unreliable and put both boat and crew in danger of perishing. The bottom of his boat was recessed to take wedge-shaped bodies which could be lifted and lowered with rods and gears either hydraulically or mechanically.

'When their flat part is lowered into the water this forms a second step. The wedge exerts lift, which

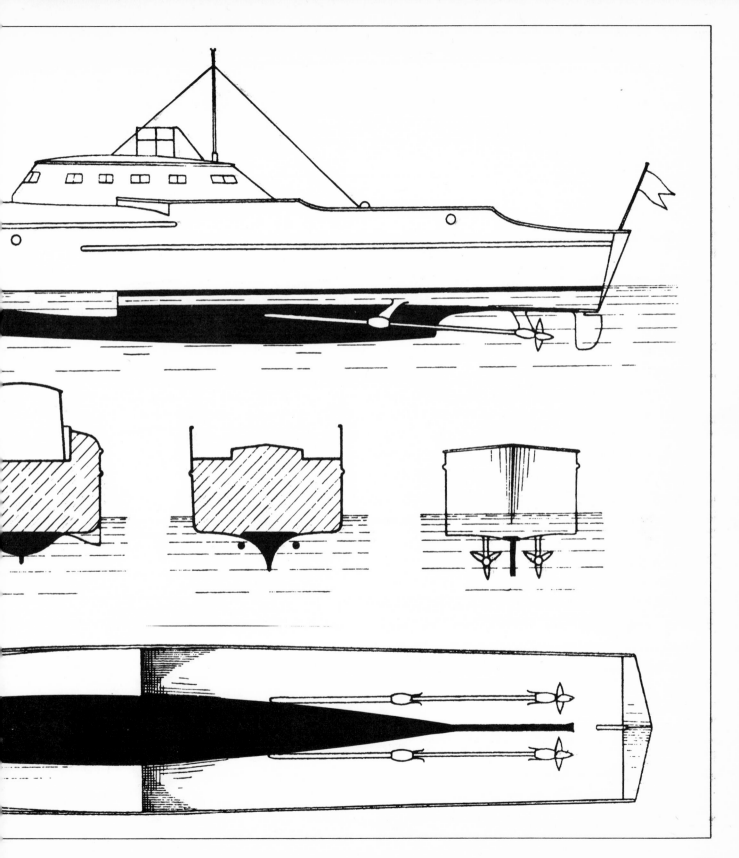

Fig. 138   Stepped planing hull by Otto Paul, Berlin, 1927
(underneath view).
Fig. 139   Stepped planing hull by Otto Paul, Berlin, 1927
(Section).
Fig. 140   Stepped planing hull by Otto Paul, Berlin, 1927
(side view).

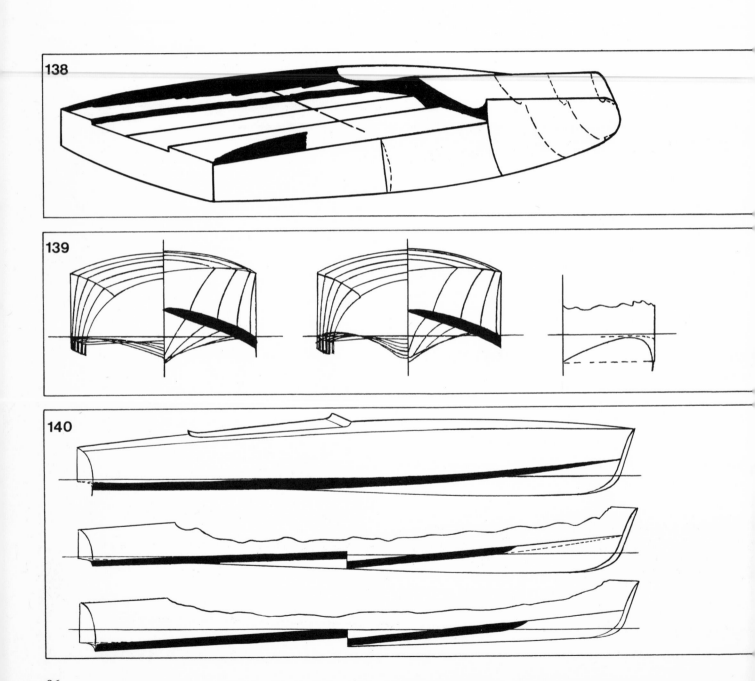

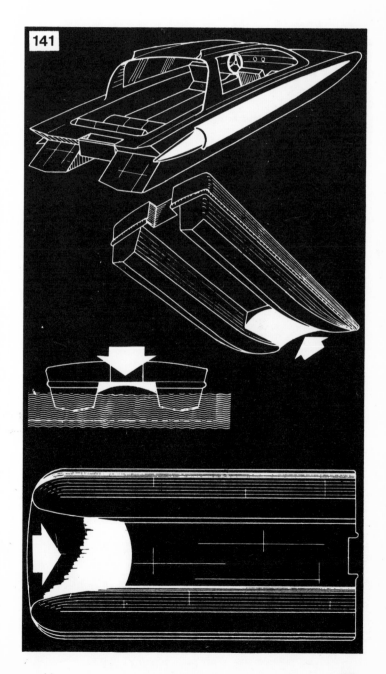

raises the bow out of the water, so that in calm water the boat can move at high speeds. When the wedge is retracted its lower surface finishes flush with the hull. The hull is then a displacement hull, which can negotiate heavy seas.' The idea obviously evolved from practical experience and is mechanically sound, but it entails the disadvantage of heavy machinery.

In 1928 Pieter van Wienen had another go at designing a stepped displacement hull which would profit from dynamic lift and thus reduce its displacement (Fig. 137). In this design the deep-V fore-section is extended into a shallow keel that runs the length of the hull to the stern. At approximately half its length there is a wide step, and from this point aft the bottom on either side of the keel is flat as in a planing hull.' But while in an ordinary planing hull the bow would lift completely out of the water at high speed, in this case the sharp edge of the keel remains immersed. Consequently the relative loss of displacement and underwater profile is not as great as it would be without the added keel.' It is interesting to compare the sections and lines of a 'fast displacement hull' or 'seagoing semi-planing hull', as we call it today, with those of van Wienen's design and see what differences have evolved in forty years.

Another design for a planing hull was patented in 1927 by Otto Paul from Berlin (Figs 138-140). With his stepped planing catamaran Paul wants to get away from wide, longitudinal steps but at the same time

Fig. 142   V-section hull with concave strake section by Ole Iver Thorsten, Woodland Hills, USA, 1965 (underneath view).

Fig. 143   V-section hull with concave strake section by Ole Iver Thorsten, Woodland Hills, USA, 1965 (side view and section).

avoid the disadvantages of a tunnelled bottom narrowing aft. His tunnelled bottom is flat aft, and at the sides sharp-edged wave-deflecting strips extend downwards. These are to prevent the water flowing through the tunnel from escaping sideways and upwards. We can recognize here, however imperfectly, the principle of the racing catamaran with a flat, stepped central platform and narrow, deep side-hulls.

This special catamaran step is also a feature of a design by René Salamin of Sierre in Switzerland (Fig. 141), which was patented in 1964. This, however, is not a *hydro*dynamic but an *aero*dynamic step, which is relatively high and extends right across the space between the two hulls. The distance between the lower edge of the step and the surface of the water is approximately equal to the height of the step, i.e. the step reduces the air gap under the forward part of the hull by half.

In conclusion let us have a look at some patented hull details. In October 1965 Ole Iver Thorsten from Woodland Hills, California, USA had the concave strakes of a V-hull with planing surfaces patented (Figs 142-143). Spray strakes as we know them today were already in use when hulls were still built of plywood in the early sixties, except that in those days they were strips glued or screwed on the outside of the hull. In plastic hulls they were laminated in but remained sharp, wedge-shaped edges. It has been established, though, that the flow of water along the bottom is

mainly concave and that these strakes interfere with it. Thorsten's V-section adapts the straked bottom to the concave flow of water—something which is easily done in a plastic moulding—and thereby reduces the

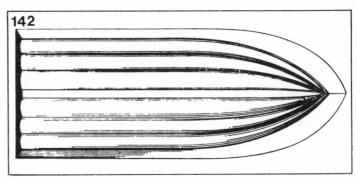

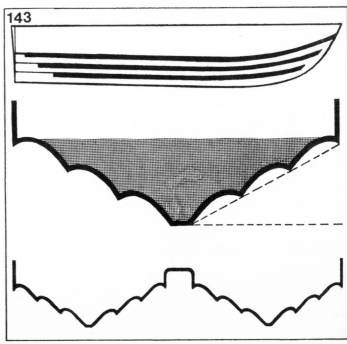

eddies otherwise formed. The angles of entrance are patented from 13° to 23°.

The more recent the patents are the greater the detail in which they are described and the longer the patent specifications. The one by which in 1966 the Chrysler Corporation of Michigan, USA applied for a patent for their well-known planing hull and which named Albert Donald Mortrude as inventor consists of thirty-seven pages and describes over seventy details (Fig. 144).

The patent concerns mainly the chine-strakes on either side. They remain above the surface of the water at slow speeds but are immersed when the boat makes a sharp turn. Their forward section is V-shaped, their after surface vertical.

As is well known, a flat-bottomed hull is fast but has little directional stability. A V-bottom, on the other hand, gives a much quieter ride and has better directional stability, but it is less suitable for planing. The aim of the Chrysler chine-strakes is to improve directional and turning stability without resorting to full-length multihulls with their high frictional resistance, and at the same time to ensure an effective foam cushion under the bottom which reduces the friction between hull and water, no matter whether the boat negotiates waves or sharp turns or moves in a relatively straight line across smooth water.

It is difficult to say exactly where the infancy of the motorboat ends and maturity begins. In man, too, this process is judged differently depending on whether he

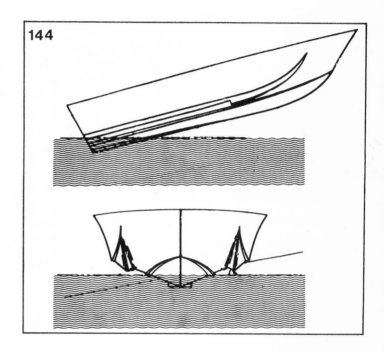

looks back on it in old-age or whether, as a young man having completed his studies and professional training, he wants to close a chapter of learning and experimenting, of high spirits and foolishness.

Let us leave it to posterity to judge exactly where the history of motorboating passes from infancy into maturity. The great follies in motorboat design may have come to an end in the 'good old times', but even some very recent ideas suggest that this branch of technology has only just outgrown its childhood days.

8 From Watershoe to Waterski

Fig. 145 Watershoe by Robert Boegel and J. Huhndorf, Breslau, Poland, 1882 (leg moving forward).

Fig. 146 Watershoe by Robert Boegel and J. Huhndorf, Breslau, 1882 (stationary leg).

Fig. 147 Watershoe by Robert Boegel and J. Huhndorf, Breslau, 1882 (front view of stationary leg).

Fig. 148 Watershoe by Robert Boegel and J. Huhndorf, Breslau, 1882 (a: flaps closed on stationary leg. b: flaps open on moving leg. c: flaps closed on stationary leg, front view).

Scarcely any other field shows the discrepancy between human dreams and technical possibilities as clearly as the story of the development of waterskis. Since time immemorial men had wanted to walk on the water, and eventually they found a way of doing so. But the effort was enormous, and there was little pleasure from it, if one compares their experience with the way we now glide over the waves or leap through the air from a ski jump.

In 1882 the two Polish inventors from Breslau, Boegel and Huhndorf patented watershoes (Figs 145-148) which they described thus—'a pair of small boats

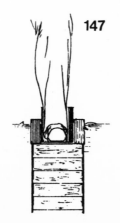

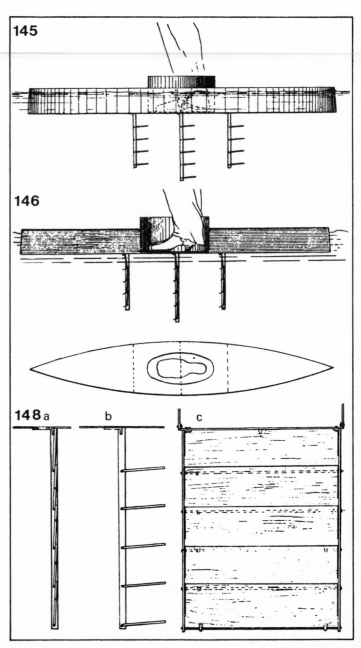

Fig. 149   Watershoes by the Viennese knight Moritz von Szabel, 1893 (with one-man crew).

Fig. 150   Watershoes by the Viennese knight Moritz von Szabel, 1893 (with two-man crew).

Fig. 151   Watershoes by the Viennese knight Moritz von Szabel, 1893 (front view with brake flaps extended on the right, folded back on the left side).

Fig. 152   Watershoes by the Viennese knight Moritz von Szabel, 1893 (top view with brake flaps extended on one shoe and folded back on the other).

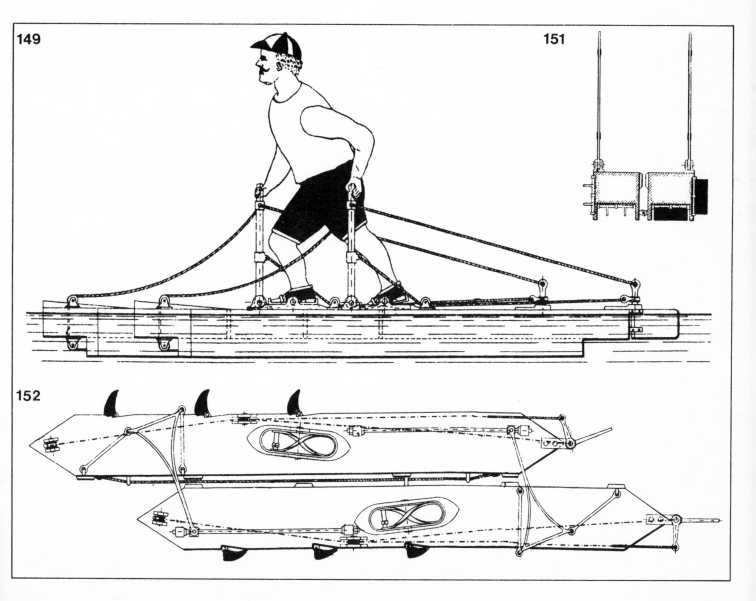

Fig. 153 Watershoes by Max Oelmann, Dresden, Germany, 1895 (top view when stationary).

Fig. 154 Watershoes by Max Oelmann, Dresden, 1895 (section when stationary).

Fig. 155 Watershoes by Max Oelmann, Dresden, 1895 (in motion).

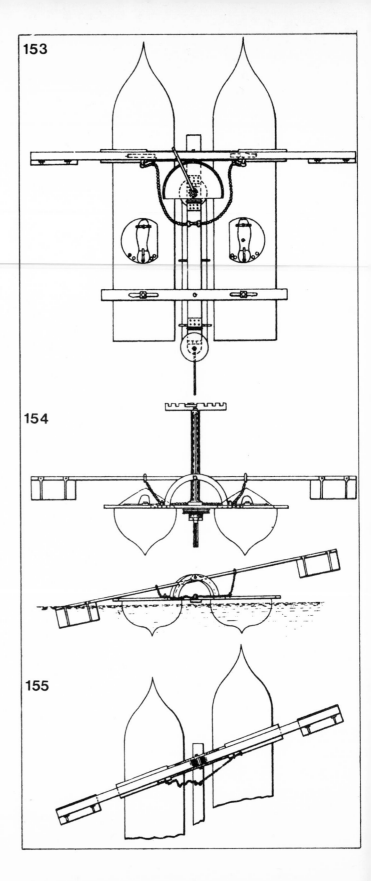

made from wood or other material, which have the ability to support a person, so that the latter, by standing with one foot in each hull can move on water as he would on land.' One foot must remain stationary while the other moves forward. To accomplish this, shutters like venetian blinds are attached underneath each foot, which are opened by the force of the water as the foot moves forward (Figs 145 and 148b) and close (Figs 146, 147, 148a etc.) when the foot comes to a standstill, so that the wearer has a fixed spot in the water. 'During long touring the tired traveller can rest on a folding stool, which is stowed in the shoes and is so arranged that the centre of gravity is not altered.'

By comparison the shoes designed by the Viennese nobleman Moritz von Szabel in 1893 (Figs 149-152) and constructed either solid or hollow from suitable materials, are a considerable improvement. Even two men could ride on them, one of them holding on to two supports, which work the rudder at the same time. The two shoes are joined together with rope and rings, so that they cannot be separated laterally. At the sides and under the keels several fins are arranged, which fold flat against the hull during movement and are extended when motion ceases (Figs 151-152). The patent extended also to the battens at the side of these fins, which were intended to channel the water. One sees clearly from the continuous attempts to hold the stationary leg effectively motionless, that watershoes were not simply improved theoretically. So the invention of Max

Fig. 156   Watershoe by Professor R. Sommer, Giessen,
Germany, 1901 (side view and top view).
Fig. 157   Watershoe by Professor R. Sommer, Giessen,
1901 (section).

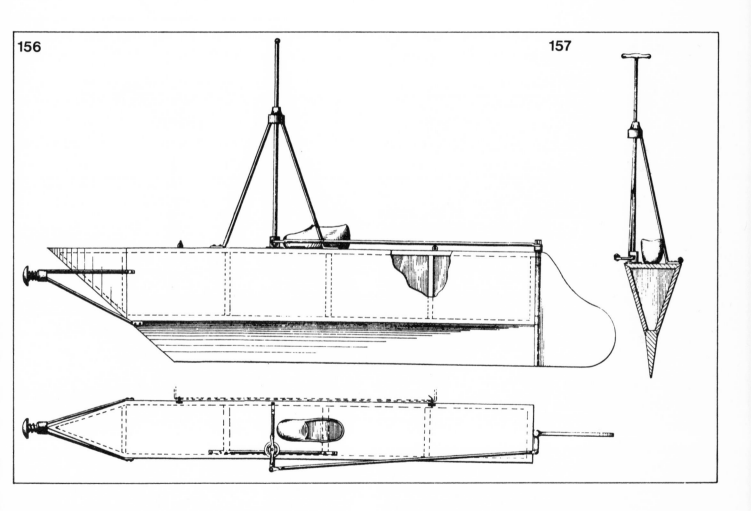

Oelmann of Dresden, Germany (Figs 153-155) consisted less in the two 'watertight wooden hulls, shaped like boats, which have a pointed bow in the front but are cut off at right angles at the back', than in the two paddles, which were pivoted athwartships and could be lowered into the water. 'As one of the hulls is pushed forward the paddle on the opposite side is pushed hard back', that is to say it stems the water and prevents the stationary foot from going backwards. 'This paddling action causes the watershoes to move forward, as has been proved in practice. The unusual shape of the paddles is to facilitate their raising and lowering in the water.' They must have been hard-boiled characters to have held such a stance with the legs wide apart and to have enough strength to paddle long distances.

The German patent of Professor Sommer from Giessen which dates from 1901 (Fig. 156) contains reference to poles, which the water walker holds and with which he operates the rudders. His invention concerns a device which controls the maximum distance between the two watershoes and at the same time allows them to move independently of each other within this limitation. 'The actual hull is made fast to the foot like a snow shoe and is very narrow for its length of two meters.' The inventor seems to have found the cross-section in the form of an isosceles triangle shown in Fig. 157 the most advantageous. 'It is advisable to fit the hull with a keel, which gives it greater stability.' Professor Sommer was also concerned about the safety of the watershoes: 'To prevent possible damage to the forward ends, buffers are fitted (Fig. 156).'

The watershoes which were invented by Richard Hoffman in the same year (Fig. 158) had a further advantage. 'The shoe conforms to all requirements and further is so arranged that it can be used on land as well.' Why should anyone want to take it easy on a walk, when it can be made harder!

This watershoe also had a keel. 'In order to get the necessary resistance to slipping backwards, each shoe has two paddlewheels, one behind the other, whose movement is so restricted by a ratchet that they turn

when the shoes move forward but lock and offer resistance if they slide back.'

As additional resistance to slipping backwards semicircular or triangular hollow cones of sheet metal are fitted to the side of the keel. They point with their tips forward, in order to cut through the water more easily in the direction of travel, but are wide at the after ends to assist the action of the paddlewheels. 'For steering

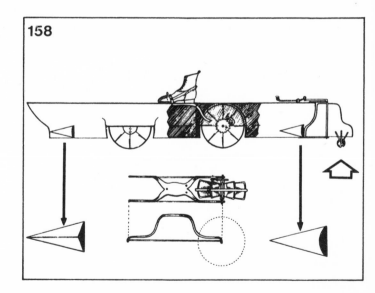

on land, the rudder of the watershoe is also used and for this purpose has a small, narrow wheel mounted underneath. This has the same resistance on land as the whole rudder in the water.'

Fig. 159 'Means of walking on water using hulls joined together' patented by Georg Krüger, Berlin, 1909.

Fig. 160 Watershoe with ballast-sack by Joseph Keiler, Munich, 1910.

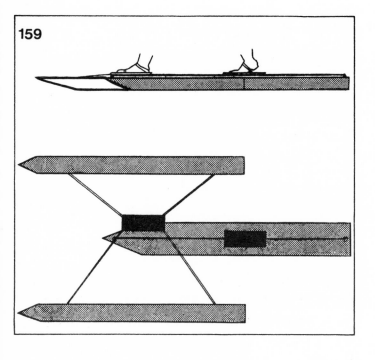

The next patents which first appeared in the patent category 'Shipbuilding and Propulsion' and then in the category 'Sport' show us very clearly the weaknesses of this incomplete mode of movement on water. Georg Krueger's 'means of walking on water using hulls joined together' appeared in 1909 and consisted of lighter hulls with shallow draft and considerably better stability. The two outer hulls, which jointly possess the same carrying capacity as the middle one, are made fast to each other with rods (Fig. 159). Midway between them is a platform for one foot, which slides along a T-shaped track on the middle ski, which takes the other foot. The distance between the feet both in a forward and sideways direction is limited. Practical? Yes—in many ways: 'Through well-known devices the apparatus for walking on water can be adapted for rowing, sitting and sailing etc.', and it can also 'be built for use by a number of people at once by providing it with the necessary number of platforms.'.

A collapsible watershoe made of cloth was invented by Josef Keiler of Munich in 1910. The patent is concerned primarily with the keel-shaped ballast sack (Fig. 160): 'Under the boat-shaped hull made of watertight cloth is placed a ballast-sack also made from cloth, which can be filled with stones and laced up.'

105

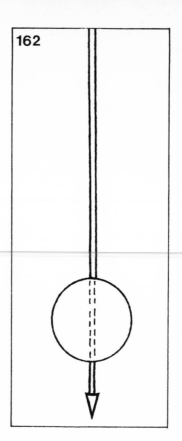

The inventor was of the opinion that this keel made it possible for the shoe to be built light and narrow without increasing the risk of capsizing. Besides, since the necessary ballast is always found plentifully near the water and hence does not have to be carried permanently in the keel, the shoes are easy to transport.

It goes without saying that anyone would want to free himself quickly from such a stone-laden appendage if the ski suddenly started to fill with water through leaking seams. He is helped in his efforts by the patented 'bindings for waterskis' invented by the brothers Starke of Grosswusterwitz (now East Germany) in 1911 (Fig. 161). 'In case of accident the skier wants to be able to free his foot from the ski with one swift movement, so that he can swim unfettered by the ski.'

In contrast to skiers on snow our brave waterski pioneers obviously kept their balance without sticks and somehow managed to slide across the water entirely without the help of their hands. A skistick for the use of waterskiers therefore was not patented until 1918 by Wilhelm Hildebrandt in Bremen, Germany (Fig. 162). Its outstanding feature is 'a hollow metal ball fitted at the lower end of the stick above an iron tip'. This is to give the wooden stick the necessary buoyancy when it is pushed down. The iron spike does not serve as a fishing harpoon but 'for pushing off when launching and fending off when coming ashore (rather like a mountain walking stick.) The stick

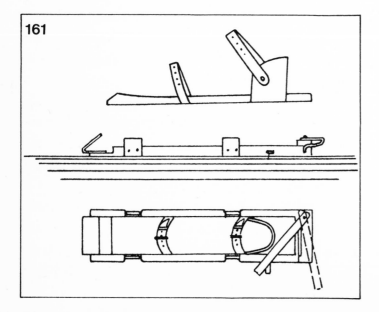

Fig.163   Pole for waterskiers with folding pressure surface by Otto Saur, Göppingen, Germany, 1923.

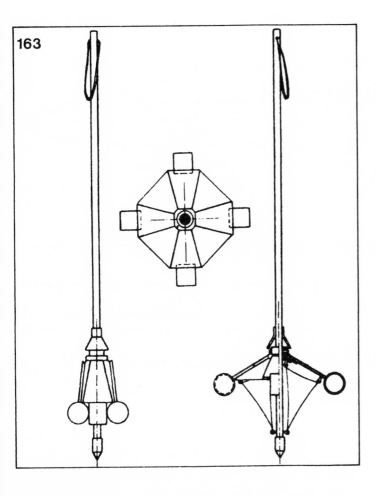

163

furthermore serves as emergency paddle in restricted and winding waters, as steering rudder, and above all as a lifebuoy. If he has an accident and ends up in the water the unfortunate waterskier instinctively hangs on to the stick and makes his way along it to the buoyant metal ball to keep his head above water.' Waterskiers

in those days do not seem to have had much faith in the seaworthiness of their skies!

Five years later, in 1923, Otto Saur from Goppingen in Germany pointed out the drawbacks of this pick-and-ball device: 'The sticks for waterskiers proposed in the past, which are intended to accelerate forward progress, to ensure the stability of the skier and act as means of steering, have at their lower end either a ball, which, because of its very shape, bounces off the water, or some flat plate, which has the disadvantage of offering considerable resistance to being retracted from the water.'

The patent of Otto Saur, shown in Fig. 163, concerns a 'ski pole for waterskiers whose collapsible pressure surfaces open out to determined limits when the pole is pushed down and close up again when it is withdrawn', and whose pressure surfaces have buoyancy tanks on their outer edges which aid the pushing and steering effects.

But let us turn back once more to the actual shoes and take a look at the 'watershoes with non-rigid hull and keel' patented by the German brothers Hermann and Paul Starke of Grosswusterwitz, which were inflated with air or gas.

The inventors had found that with inflatable watershoes the area immediately beneath the foot was excessively depressed, so that movement was unsteady and unsafe and the life of the watershoe was shortened due to quicker wear.

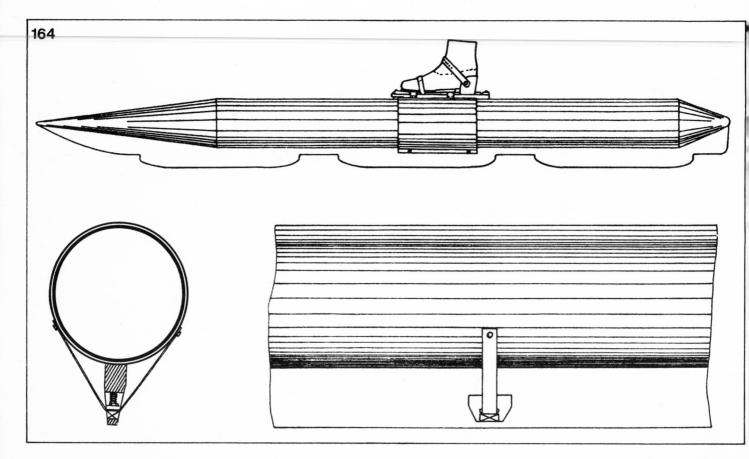

In their design the pressure of the foot comes onto a rigid cylinder made fast to the keel, and an additional patent covers 'two struts which brace the keel against the hull and are made fast on either side of the hull' (Fig. 164). One might call this a miniature inflatable boat with one tube for each foot but with a wood or metal keel and the problem of attaching this to an inflatable rubber or fabric body.

The future certainly lay on the water, but comfort was some way off. Karl Ligotzki from Berlin, Germany made an effort in 1917 to improve things by inventing (Fig. 165) 'telescopic legs with ball joints which link the shoes fore and aft with a metal ring which supports the body of the rider without hampering his freedom of movement.'

On each shoe there are two perpendicular flaps which

open out against the water flow if the shoes are driven backwards. Apart from having my feet strapped down I do not think I should have liked to be chained in the ring! The distance between the outstretched legs is astounding. It must have been a powerful giant to have his feet so far apart and still be able to do energetic exercise!

A glimpse into the interior of a watershoe is afforded by the patent of Josef Keiler and Anton Mössmer of Munich, Germany (1912). The invention concerns a collapsible frame (Fig. 166), which consists of rings over which is stretched a wooden skin. The apparatus can be collapsed without having to be taken apart by simply pushing the rings together. The form of con-

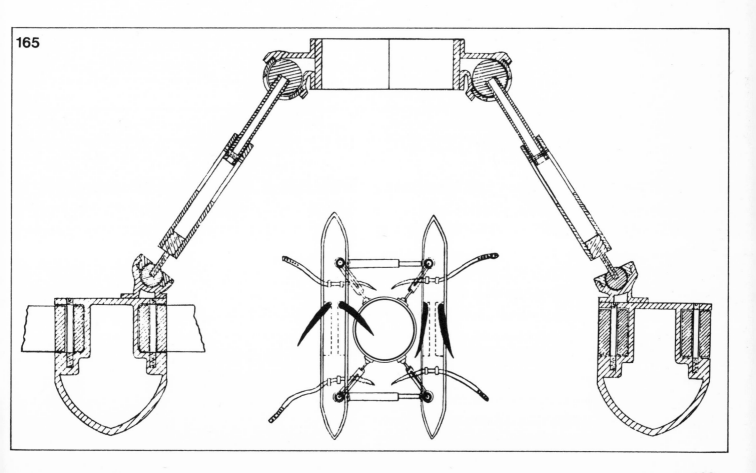

165

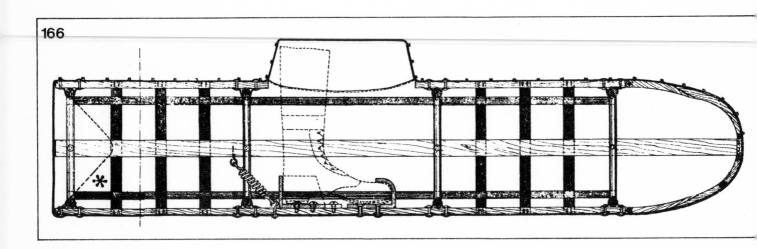

struction is not only protected for watershoes but also for water velocipedes, water sleighs, folding boats, lifeboats and other vessels.

By comparison the 'device for moving on the water with floats attached to the feet' patented in 1919 by Victor Jasinski from Gdingen in Poland could almost be called a walking boat. The floats attached to the feet slide in tracks on a platform with a seat on top. By sitting on this seat, which is adjustable in height, the person using it holds the craft steady, and 'besides, the seat allows the person to rest' (Fig. 167)! Obviously a vehicle with greater stability, but it is doubtful whether it could be got to move.

In the same year Eugen Schäfer of Hamburg, Germany, took out a patent for watershoes which are obviously intended for high speeds. Basically, they

consist of a number of shallow floats (Fig. 168) one behind the other and linked by a flexible framework with a platform on top, on which the foot rests. The joints between the floats and the framework are so flexible that by pushing down with the foot they 'are

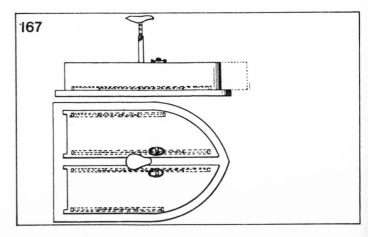

Fig. 168 Watershoe with platform and flexible framework by Eugen Schäfer, Hamburg, Germany, 1919.

Fig. 169 Watershoes with rudders by Kurt Erfurt, Berlin, 1924.

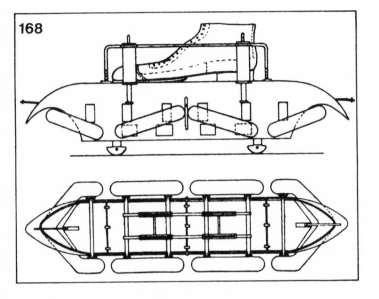

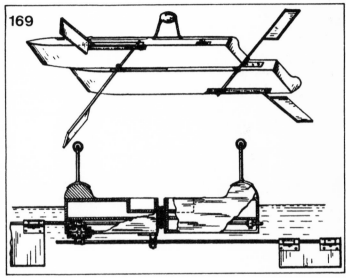

set into a swinging motion which enhances the buoyancy of the floats and ensures that with each step the foot has the necessary support.'

In addition to the side floats there are further floats fore and aft, which not only help balance but act as wave deflectors. According to the inventor his shoes could also be used for walking on land. He did not say what advantage there was to be derived from this—perhaps one could jump on them as on a spring?

In 1924 Kurt Erfurt from Berlin patented a device for 'higher speed in a straight direction', which consisted of two boat-shaped floats alongside each other. 'The user stands with each foot in the foot-well of one hull (Fig. 169) and supports himself on hand-holds [placed astonishingly low]. As the person advances the right foot, the forward set of rudders with the two rudder blades attached to each float exerts a constant rudder pressure . . . Since the after pair of rudders is attached to the floats the other way round to the forward set, they move simultaneously in the opposite direction.' The process is no more complicated than it is to understand it!

Compared to this 'fully automatic' and hence inherently trouble-prone device, the manually operated apparatus designed by Otto Bruman of Zürich, Switzerland, in 1928 appears surprisingly reliable (Fig. 170).

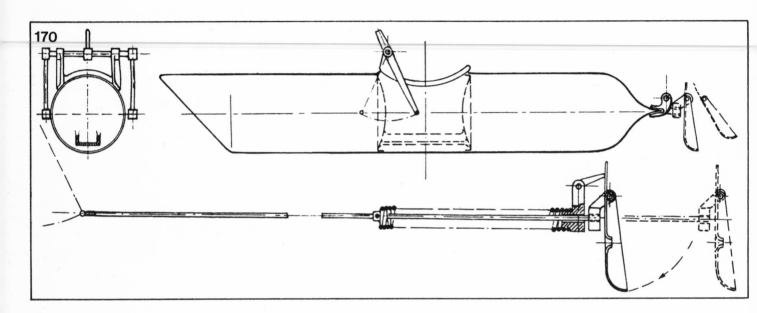

'Automatic brake flaps are well known', we read in the patent specification by Mr Bruman's design office. 'They have the disadvantage, however, that half the braking action is lost before they come fully into operation, so that progress is only very slow.' This brake flap is so arranged that it can be operated by hand with each step. It consists of a flap at the stern held in position by a hand lever via a spring and is raised by releasing the spring as the foot is moved forward. Amazing what design offices got up to fifty years ago.

It was only in 1933 that people began to think of watershoes as being related to skis. The German,

Erwin Sessler patented a 'device for turning skis into watershoes' by enclosing each ski in a watertight sheath (Figs 171 and 172). This consists of an inflatable section and a pocket for inserting the ski. For the first time the skis, which are rather narrow, are kept apart at the correct distance by a tubular frame reaching up to waist height. This can be folded down when not in use. In order to prevent the waterskis from going backwards they are fitted on their outer edges with rubber pockets with openings facing aft, which fill up with water if the skis move backwards, thus providing resistance.

The first real waterski patent was taken out by two

112

Fig. 171 'Device for turning skis into watershoes' by Erwin Sessler, Herzberg, Germany, 1933. The arrows indicate the funnel-shaped rubber pockets which act as resistance against moving backwards.
Fig. 172 'Device for turning skis into watershoes' by Erwin Sessler, Herzberg, 1933 (details).
Fig. 173 Patented waterski by Max Neumann and Wilhelm Jaburek, Heidenau and Pirna in Saxony, 1935.

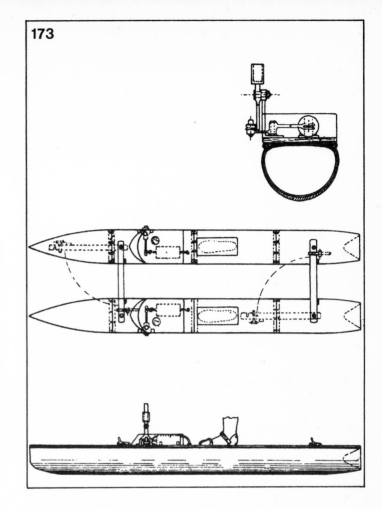

Germans, Max Neuman from Heidenau and Wilhelm Jaburek from Pirna on the Elbe in 1935. This ski is also a displacement model (Fig. 173) but already conceived in modern form. The inflatable part which, similar to a car tyre, is made of an outer tube and an inner tube with a valve on it, is topped with a thin foot-board. This is attached by the method used for car tyres, i.e. there are rims under the boards and beaded edges to the inflatable hulls. The skis are inflated and the pressure regulated during use by a manometer and a hand pump fixed to the foot-board. Technical perfection in the wrong place.

This array of curious pre-war waterski patents is brought to a close by the spray guard designed by Harald Strohmeier from Austria. His patent once again highlights the shortcomings from which this displacement type of waterski suffered and which were only overcome twenty years later by the planing waterski.

'Making the foot opening in watershoes watertight is an important matter, for the reserve of buoyancy in such vessels is not great, is they are not to be too clumsy. On longer tours the skier can, therefore, be endangered by leakage into the shoes. The invention consists of a spray guard (Fig. 174), which is not only watertight but in the case of an accident automatically released from the float without the need to undo buckles or laces.'

In all the watershoes described so far the footwell has either been completely open or protected by an attached cuff. In inflatable watershoes the top edge of this

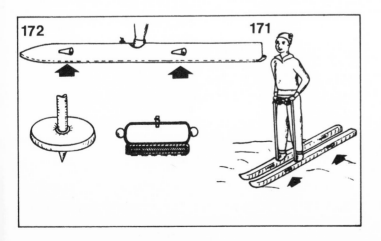

174

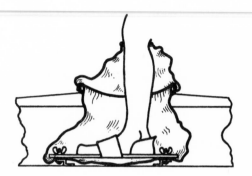

cuff had to be wide enough for the framework to be passed through every time they were set up or dismantled. 'In rigid watershoes, too, the opening has to be at least wide enough to pass gear through and to insert one arm and one foot simultaneously when making them fast', Strohmeier writes in his patent specification. 'Since the sleeve, for this reason, has to have a fairly wide opening at the top, it could never be made completely watertight.'

Well, despite these problems over a watertight rubber cuff for the foot-well, the development of watershoes progressed steadily towards our modern planing water-ski.

The waterski as we know it today was born in the late forties on the other side of the Atlantic, and many still believe that there was a direct transition from the water or ice-ski, which is similar in size and shape. To think that the many types of hydrodynamic planing skis which are now in use had such clumsy ancestors, which could be made to move across the water only with great effort and much auxiliary gear! Only the waterski-helicopter still reminds us of them. At rest or at slow speeds it, too, is a displacement craft. Powerful engines not only make it plane but even fly. What was a mere dream to the early water-walkers has finally come true.

9 In Case of Shipwreck

Fig. 175 'Mattress to be used as life-saving device in case of shipwreck' by Charles J. Pigeon and Louis Lacroix, Paris, 1888 (top view showing how the centre panels are pushed apart).
Fig. 176 'Mattress to be used as life-saving device in case of shipwreck' by Charles J. Pigeon and Louis Lacroix, Paris, 1888 (top view showing the fold-back panel).

The history of life-saving devices has brought forth as many serious, workable inventions as it has ridiculous ones. We are surprised to find that many principles of safety at sea, which are still valid today, were already put into practice in those early days and that inventions patented fairly recently are based on ideas already patented two or three generations ago. We also recognize the misfortune of some inventors, whose ideas could not be put into practice on a commercial scale because technology was not sufficiently advanced and the necessary materials had not yet been developed. We cannot help but laugh at many patents which were certainly meant to be taken seriously in the times of which they were born and, indeed, *were* taken seriously by their inventors, who, after all, had to pay a sizable fee.

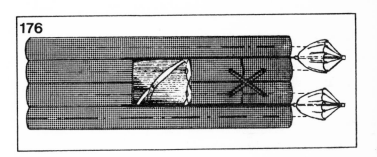

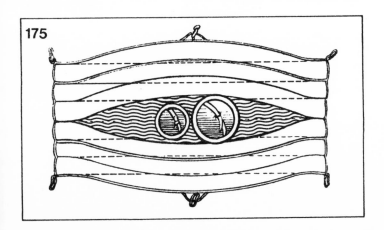

Let us first take a look at some items of gear, which were normally intended for daily use on board and only in second place as life-saving devices.

In 1888 Charles J. Pigeon and Louis Lacroix of Paris took out a patent on a 'mattress to be used as life-saving device in case of shipwreck'. This inflatable mattress, which was made up of four or more airtight cylinders that could be inserted into a cover to make them more comfortable to lie on, was intended for normal use in a bunk or suspended from a bamboo or metal frame. In case of emergency the centre panels could be pushed apart (Fig. 175) or folded back (Fig. 176) to expose a watertight sack, which was weighted with lead and fitted with webbed feet. Into this the shipwrecked mariner stepped and jumped overboard (Fig. 177). One great advantage of the mattress was that mothers could seat their small children in the well in front of them and thus keep an eye on them (Fig. 178).

Fig. 177 'Mattress to be used as life-saving device in case of shipwreck' by Charles J. Pigeon and Louis Lacroix, Paris, 1888 (section, as used by a shipwrecked man).

Fig. 178 'Mattress to be used as life-saving device in case of shipwreck' by Charles J. Pigeon and Louis Lacroix, Paris, 1888 (side view, with shipwrecked mother and child).

177

'The sulphur contained in the rubber (of which the mattress was made) has no harmful effect on people', the inventor hurriedly points out. 'Quite on the contrary, it successfully combats the bacteria of typhoid, cholera and other infections. Because of these advantages it can be highly recommended.'

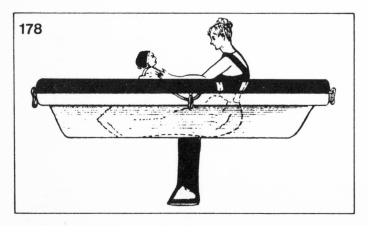

178

Equally useful was the 'Lifebuoy in the shape of a suitcase' (Fig. 179), which Paul Kränkel of Leipzig had patented in September 1891. Indispensable both for voyages on big ships and on small yachts, this suitcase had 'an opening in the lid and the base, which is normally closed by a lid or a slide, and a rigid cylinder, which forms a tube passing through the middle of the case. In case of emergency the user steps into this, pulls the suitcase up under his arms and jumps into the water. The air contained in the case keeps him afloat in an upright position.'

The rigid, telescopic tube 'for the purpose of accommodating the person's legs and at the same time protecting them' could be filled with personal belongings, as could the rest of the suitcase when it was not in use in the water.

Next time we have guests on board we had better take a good look at their suitcases to see whether, perhaps, there is a nervous type among them who secretly distrusts our ship or our navigation!

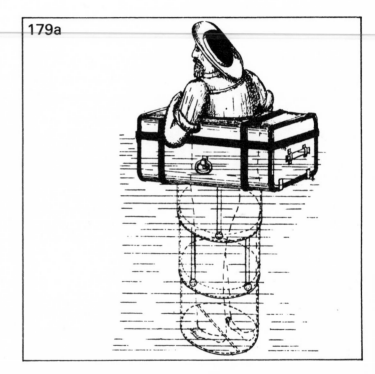

179a

Anyone carrying the patented suitcase by the German, Adolf Dette (1899), on the other hand, shows himself quite openly to be a coward. The four sides of this box

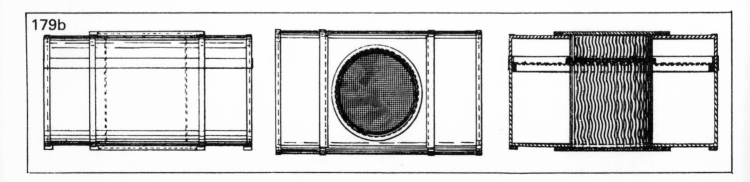

179b

Fig. 180   Life-saving suitcase by the German Adolf Dette, of Sondershausen, 1899 (collapsed).

Fig. 181   Life-saving suitcase by Adolf Dette, Sondershausen, 1899 (unfolded for use).

Fig. 182   Folding chair which converts into life-raft by Louis Röder and Johannes Meyer, Hamburg, Germany, 1903 (shown for sitting on).

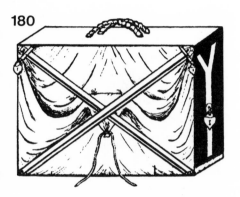

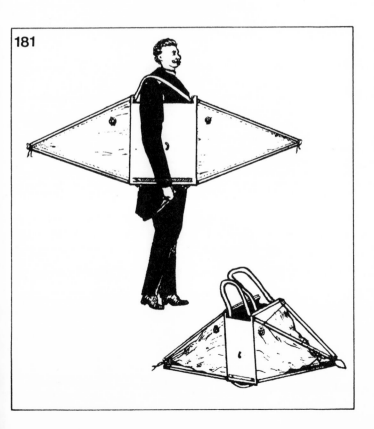

made of waterproof material form a rigid frame, while its top and bottom can be removed (Fig. 180). To two of the sides there is attached a kind of sack, which, when the case is in normal use, is folded up against the side with metal braces. In case of emergency these are unfolded to make a supporting framework for the sacks, which are inflated and tied to the apex of the frame (Fig. 181). A special advantage of these carefully designed inflatable sacks, which anyone will appreciate when swimming ashore from his wrecked ship, lies in their low form resistance.

Quite realistic, by comparison, is the 'fixing device for detachable seats of deck-chairs and the like used as life-saving gear' designed by Louis Röder and Jo-

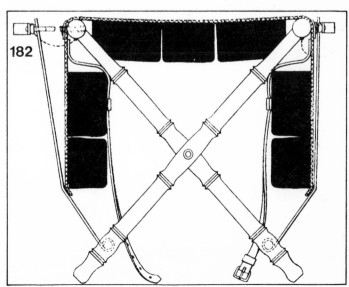

Fig. 183 Folding chair which converts into life-raft by Louis Röder and Johannes Meyer, Hamburg, 1903 (shown dismantled for use as life-raft).

Fig. 184 Folding chair which converts into life-raft by Matthias Kuhnen and August Spader, New York, 1905 (as chair).

Fig. 185 Folding chair which converts into life-raft by Matthias Kuhnen and August Spader, New York, 1905 (as life-raft).

hannes Meyer of Hamburg, Germany, in 1903 (Fig. 182). The lifebelt, which forms the seat of a folding chair, is made of a square of sailcloth on the underside of which there are attached pieces of cork sewn up in sailcloth, empty tins or other very buoyant objects. The patent is particularly concerned with the attachment of this seat to the chair by a number of special fittings (Fig. 183).

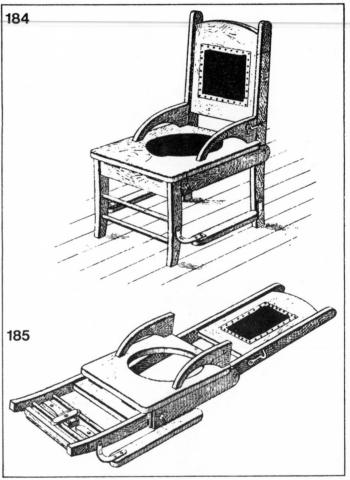

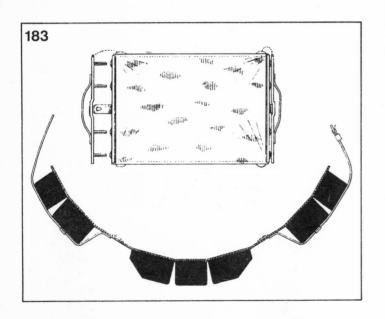

By comparison the attempt by Matthias Kuhnen and August Spader of New York in 1905 to adapt a deck-chair as life-raft (Fig. 184) appears clumsy. This was to be done by folding the upholstered back-rest backwards and the seat cushion, which is part of a separate panel under the seat, forward. This exposes an opening in the seat, into which the shipwrecked person climbs and supports himself by the handles on either side (Fig. 185). It could hardly have provided him with much additional buoyancy!

Figs 186a and 186b   Life-suit which folds up into a pillow by Hanseatische Apparatebau GmbH, Kiel, Germany, 1917.

186a

life-suits about in those days, which, together with the attached life-belt, took up a great deal of room. We shall have a look at one of these monstrosities later. 'This invention makes it possible to carry a life-suit for every person on board and stow it so that it is easily accessible.' The life-belt is so shaped that with the suit folded up it makes a wedge-shaped pillow for use in a bunk or the cockpit. The suit is made of waterproof material and attached all round to the belt, which is slightly higher and thicker at the back 'to ensure that the user takes up the best position in the water'. Obviously the inventor never tried his own inventions, for if he had he would have found that after a while he got his nose rather wet, because the extra buoyancy at the back makes the wearer float on his stomach!

A comparatively recent invention is the special sea-boot patented by the Englishman Arnold Louis How-

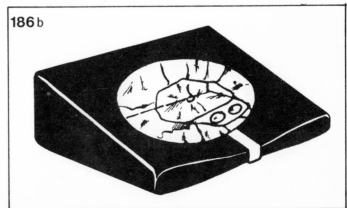

186b

The Hanseatische Apparatebau GmbH of Kiel in Germany in 1917 brought out a complete life-suit that folded up into a pillow (Figs 186a and 186b). There were, in fact, quite a number of very unwieldy

Fig. 187   Buoyant sea-boot by Arnold Louis Howarth,
England, 1930.

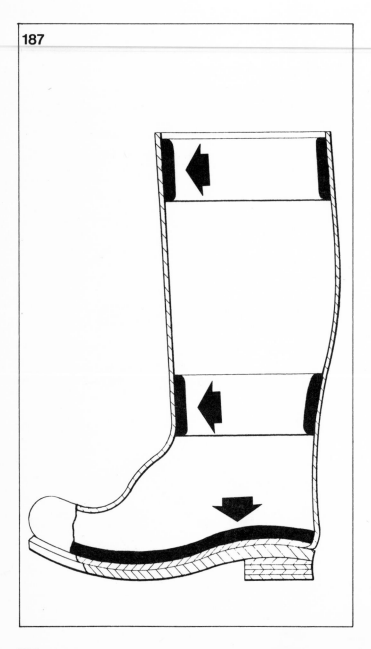

187

arth in 1930 (Fig. 187). 'It is well known', he says, 'that if a man falls overboard wearing ordinary sea-boots these will interfere with his efforts to swim because of their weight, so that after a short time he is in danger of drowning from fatigue. The aim of my invention is to prevent this.'

The inventor recommends the use of some buoyant material as an inner sole, round the ankles and at the top of the boot, thereby giving it roughly the same specific weight as that of water. In this way the boot will be practically weightless in the water. At the same time Howarth warns of making it too buoyant and thus lifting the wearer's feet dangerously high in the water.

Admittedly, heavy leather boots that reached up to the hips were a danger for every man on deck. But rubber knee-boots, like most other clothes worn on board, are neutral in weight and always trap some air, no matter whether trousers are worn inside or out. If they are in the way they can always be pulled off in an emergency, even if this means cold feet in the long run. There is certainly no call for Mr Howarth's boots nowadays.

The earliest models of personal buoyancy were made up of rigid components, either solid or hollow. It was a problem to remain agile in these unwieldy and uncomfortable pieces of gear, which had to be worn for all work on deck. J. Johansen of Copenhagen, Denmark tried to overcome this problem with his 'new type of safety gear for crew and passengers' patented in 1880

Fig. 188 'New type of safety gear' by J. Johannsen, Copenhagen, Denmark, 1880 (in carrying case and as worn by a person).
Fig. 189 'New type of safety gear' by J. Johannsen, Copenhagen, 1880 (close-up).

(Fig. 188). This 'apparatus, which does not interfere with the crew in the normal execution of their duties in lifeboats and other small and large vessels, but which will save them from drowning if they should go overboard' consists of twelve cork pieces of different shapes and sizes held together by linen straps (Fig. 189).

The way the buoyancy is divided up undoubtedly gives the wearer maximum freedom of movement, and the weight of nearly 8 lbs is more than adequate, but the concentration of buoyancy at the back certainly would

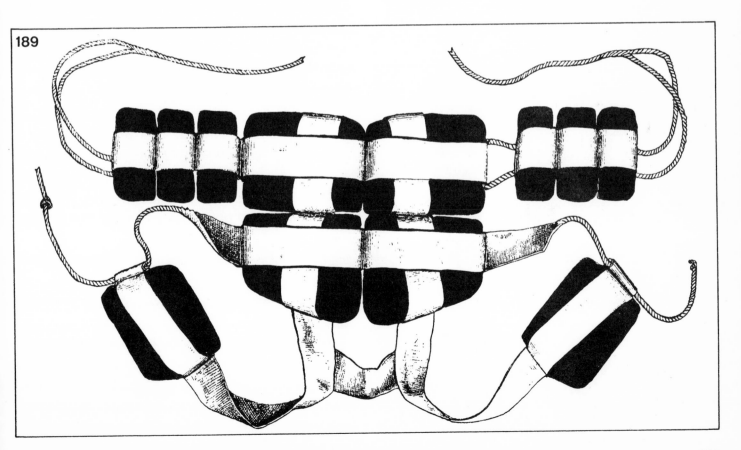

not result in the wearer 'adopting a vertical position in the water so that the head and part of the shoulders remain above water'. This assumption is completely erroneous, yet for decades life-jackets were designed according to it. Some of them still are to this day!

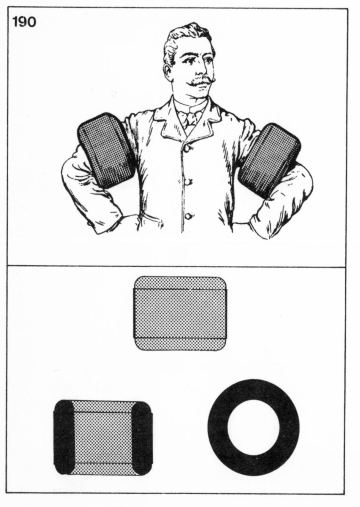

190

An invention by the two Italians Silvio Occhiale and Salomone Sinigalia of Turin, which was patented in 1899, is strikingly advanced by comparison. In very slightly modified form it is still in use today as swimming and buoyancy aid for children (Fig. 190). These inflatable arm rings were very light and held a large volume of air. Besides offering maximum freedom of movement they took into account a new and important realization, namely that 'above all, previous types of personal buoyancy could not be worn high enough on the body to keep the head and breathing organs above water in the correct manner'. The two Italians intended to overcome this problem with this new type of buoyancy, which not only had an unconventional shape but was also worn in an unusual place.

It never became popular when it was first patented, but at least its inventors had their efforts recognized posthumously. Their patent specification, which describes 'a device for saving a person in the water, consisting of hollow bodies with rounded rims, which can be worn round the upper arms without any means of fastening and which, due to the water pressure against them when the wearer makes swimming movements with his arms, have the tendency to rise above the water' needed only slight modification to describe the type of buoyancy wings which are now patented in many countries and are very widely used.

The great-grandfather of our one-man canoe is undoubtedly the collapsible craft patented as life-saving

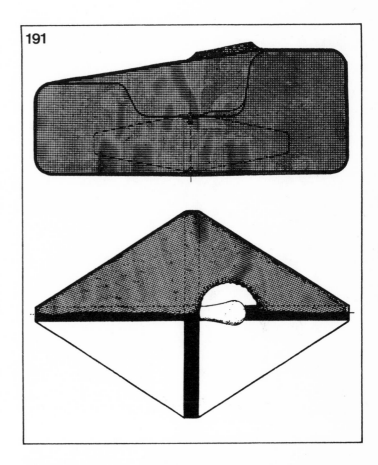

device by J. Gutknecht of Zürich, Switzerland, in 1900 (Fig. 191). It consists of two frames, one of which is slotted into the other at right angles and turns round a bolt. These frames support a cover of waterproof cloth. The result is an enclosed space with an opening, which can be closed fairly tightly round the upper part of the body by means of a drawstring. Not the ideal lifeboat, but probably no less safe than a folding canoe. It folds flat (when not in use) and takes up very little stowage space.

It is certainly more confidence-inspiring than the 'sausage seller' in Fig. 192, who is wearing a string of cork shapes sewn up in rubberized cloth and covered with soot to make them water-repellent. 'The individual cylinders are tied off with tarred twine and impregnated to make them water-repellent and non-inflammable. The person wearing the device can be either clothed or naked.'

Indeed, this invention by Frederic Holthausen of Clichy-La-Garenne in France, patented in 1900, incorporates a number of advantages which are not immediately apparent from the amusing pictures. The hooks at the ends could be fastened to eyes anywhere between two pieces of cork, and in this way the device can be made to fit tightly round the wearer's body without hampering his mobility. Most of the corks (perhaps unintentionally) are arranged on his chest, so that he floats in the position which sixty years later was recognized as the only safe one. It is safe even if the wearer becomes unconscious. So our sausage-seller from France was, in fact, more enlightened at the turn of the century than many safety experts were fifty years later, who tried all their lives to design the ideal life-jacket and never succeeded.

The lifebelt patented in 1904 for Franz Karl Parizot of Bremen, Germany, (Figs 193a and 193b) is similarly effective. Round the inner rim it has an elastic collar

125

Figs. 192a and 192b   String of rubber-covered cork pieces to be used as life-saving device. By Frederic Holthausen, France, 1900.

Figs. 193a and 193b   Buoyancy collar by Franc Karl Parizot, Bremen, Germany, 1904.

192b

192a

The 'device to be worn on the back by persons in the water', which was patented in 1904 by the firm of E. Fröhlich of Breslau, Poland, (Figs 194a and 194b) is something of a joke. Made of sheet metal and shaped so that it narrows in precisely the place where it ought to provide maximum buoyancy, it might have been taken from a cartoonist's sketch book, complete with its bearded wearer.

Let us continue in the comical vein for a moment and take a look at some of the 'life-suits' which it was fashionable to patent in those early days. Figs 195, 196 and 196a show 'a life-suit consisting of top and trousers, the top having tape loops at the front and a pocket at the back for stowing provisions, valuables or distress flares and being made up of five separate air chambers.'

which, when pulled over the head, will fit snugly round the user's neck. In those days the ring was filled with cork or kapok, but when it was revived quite recently it was made inflatable and of rubberized material. Its advantage is that, unlike most other devices featured here, it provides buoyancy in the right place, even if the elastic collar under the wearer's chin could not have been very comfortable.

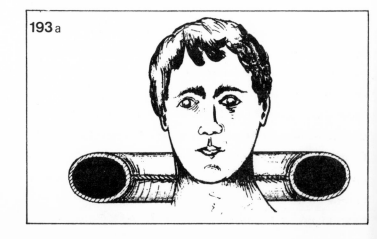

193a

Figs. 194a and 194b   'Device to be worn by persons in the water' by E. Fröhlich, Breslau, Poland, 1904.

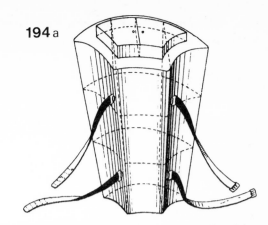

194a

194b

gentlemen only in that the trouser legs are much wider at the top in order to accommodate ladies' dresses without difficulty. Besides, they have a third strap to hold the clothes together.' I wonder whether, in an emergency, a gentleman might have been pursuaded to wear a lady's suit if it was the only one available. Or would he rather have drowned?

The invention by E. Frankenberg of Hannover, Ger-

193.b

This 'astronaut's suit' designed by Senor Salvador Malo y Valdivielso of Paris in 1888 had inflatable pockets at the front and back as well as in the sleeves and enclosing the head. These could be inflated by a tube and valve. The claws at the end of the sleeves, which remind us of a robot, were worked by the hands from inside. The inventor proposed two slightly different suits for ladies (Figs 196a and 196b) and gentlemen (Fig. 195).

'The trousers intended for ladies differ from those for

many, (1896) concerns merely 'a number of improvements to the well-known life-suits which enclose the whole person, with their equally well-known air-pockets and weighted soles. These improvements aim at maintaining an even temperature inside the suit, admitting fresh air and expanding the suit in order to accommodate several persons.'

The suit is, as usual, made of waterproof material. To prevent the air space from being compressed by the

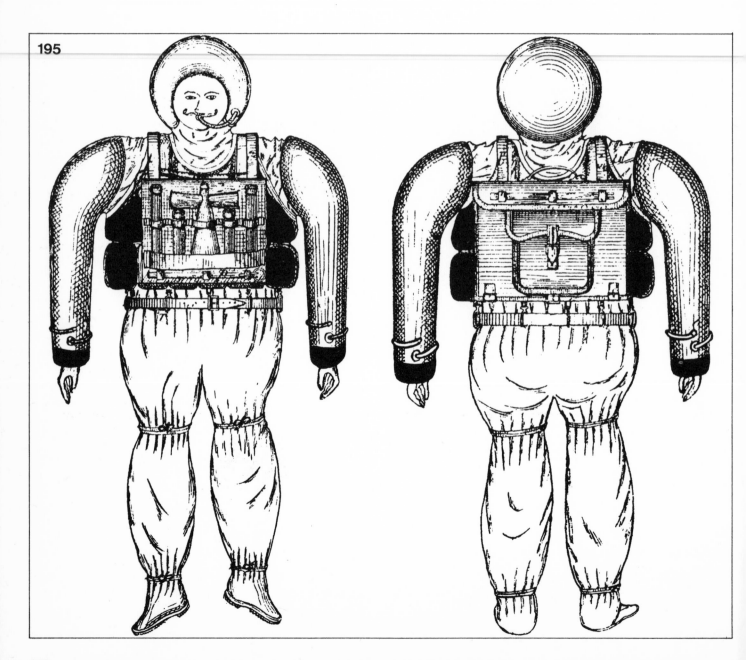

195

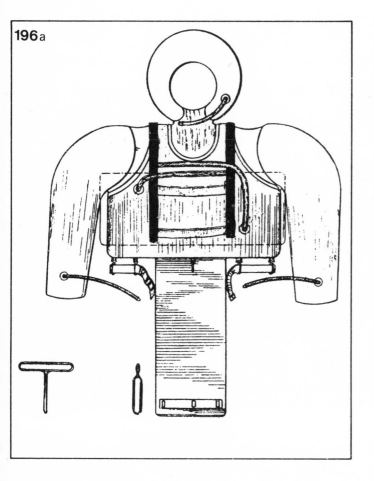

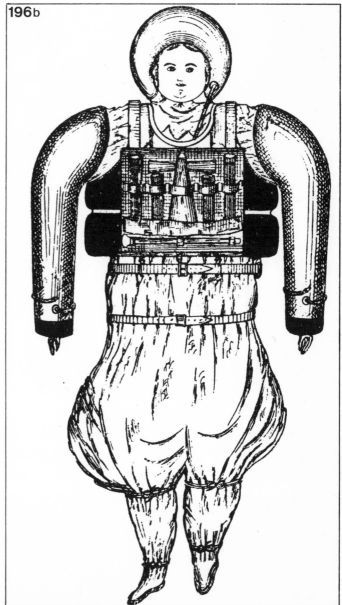

water pressure, wicker hoops have been fitted. Fig. 197 shows the patented helmet of the suit, which has 'an opening for the intake and expulsion of air in the lid above the person's head. This ensures a warm temperature and affords protection against the cold from outside.' The breathing tube is bent downwards to prevent water getting inside the helmet. Why the air should be warmer above the person's head than in front of his nose the inventor, alas, does not say.

He also had a variation on the theme patented (Figs 198 and 199), in which 'with the aim of increasing the volume of air surrounding the body the watertight cloth enclosure is enlarged into a box shape above the knee and sealed with a harmonica-type lid (with access hatch), so that, if necessary, several persons can be accommodated.' There was only leg-room for one, though!

A great step forward was the 'collapsible lifebuoy with attached watertight suit' invented by the Geneva firm of Probst & Philippon in 1900 (Figs 200-203). It has a number of striking advantages: it is attached to the life-rail of the boat and ready for use at any time. The life-suit, which is made of soft leather with sleeves, cuffs, helmet with window and ventilation hole, folds up into the life-buoy (Fig. 200).

The buoy is thrown to the man overboard, who releases two fastenings, climbs into the suit (Fig. 201) and closes the helmet. While he is on the look-out for his rescuers, who, we hope, have not forgotten him, he

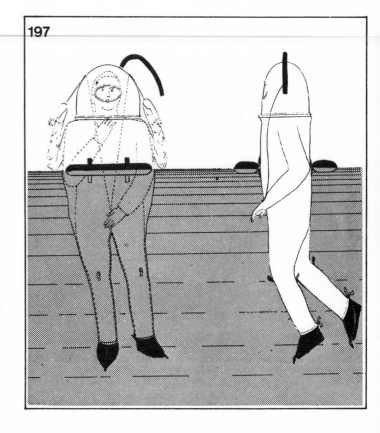

can either stand or sit (Fig. 202). If he has to wait a rather long time he can even lie down in the suit and have forty winks (Fig. 203): 'The suit has a full-length airtight partition, which together with the back of the suit forms an airtight chamber. This can be inflated with air or some other suitable gas if the suit is to be used for lying on the water.' The inventor has not forgotten a seat and a rope ladder for supporting the

These patented life-suits were actually made. Here their efficiency is tested in the Alster at Hamburg in Germany at the turn of the century.

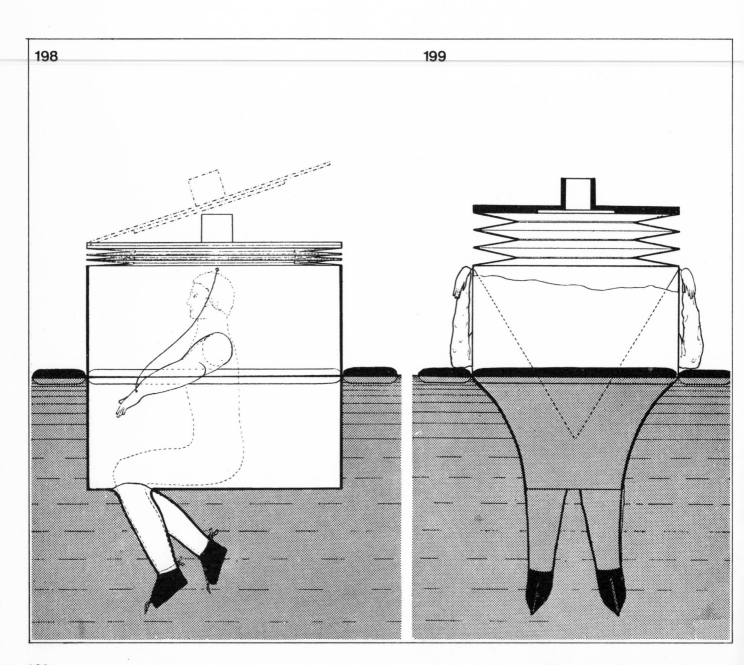

Fig. 198 Floating box by E. Frankenberg, Hannover, Germany, 1896 (side view).

Fig. 199 Floating box by E. Frankenberg, Hannover, 1896 (section).

198

199

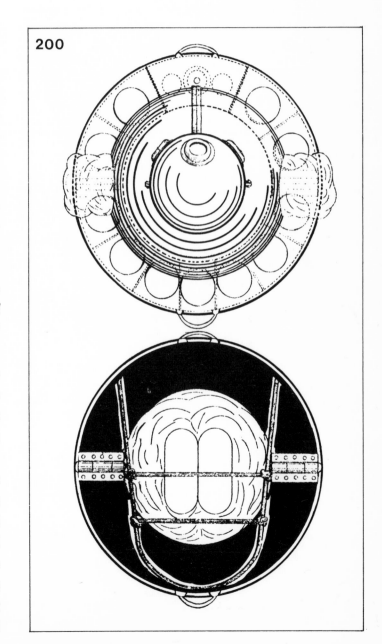

200

feet (Fig. 202), so that our shipwrecked mariner can enjoy even a prolonged stay in the water in comfort.

But let us return to inventions of rather more lasting importance. As long ago as 1880 three German gentlemen from Kiel by the name of Johannsen, Schmielau and Arp had the idea of making a waistcoat of two layers of rubberized linen sewn together to form channels, into which cork was inserted (Figs 204a and 204b). They had realized not only that this coat would enclose the body snugly yet flexibly but also that the air spaces formed by the corrugated surface of the coat would allow the skin to breathe.

Bernhard Liedtke of Königsberg, Germany went one step further by filling a life-jacket with *carbonized cork* with a specific weight of 0.080 instead of ordinary cork with a specific weight of 0.238 (Fig. 205). This means that only about one third of the quantity has to be used. A further advantage lies in the fact that carbonized cork absorbs much less water than ordinary cork and retains its original buoyancy even after several days in the water.

Bernhard Liedtke was the first to calculate how much buoyancy a person needed: 'From the aforegoing figures regarding the specific weight of carbonized cork we deduce that 1 kilogram (2.2 lbs) of carbonized cork can support a load of 10 to 12 kilograms in the water. A man in heavy clothes (including sturdy boots and loaded pockets) and immersed in the water so far that he can still breathe weighs approximately 3.5

Fig. 201 Probst & Philippon's collapsible lifebuoy with
the life-suit unfolded and the helmet opened.

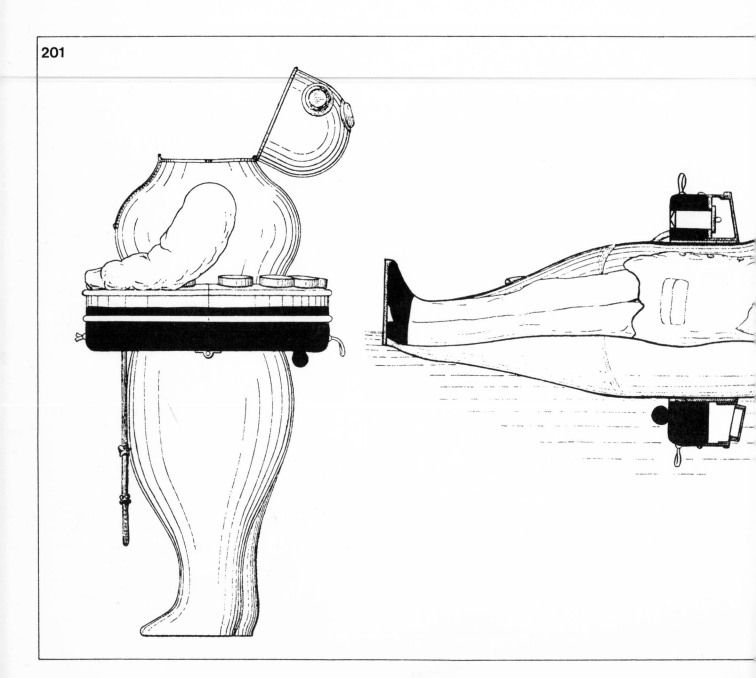

201

Fig. 202   A man could even lie down and go to sleep in the collapsible lifebuoy by Probst & Philippon.

Fig. 203   Alternatively, he could stand upright or sit down.

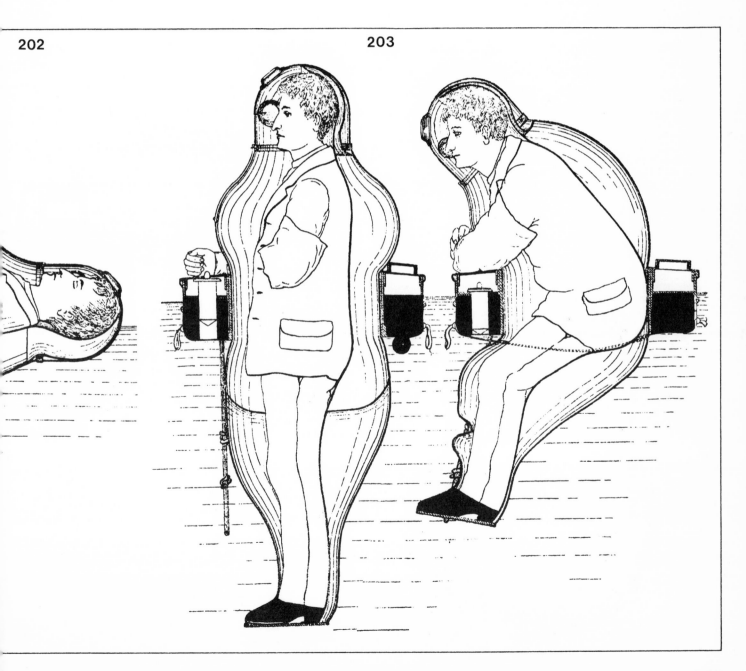

202

203

kilograms (7.7 lbs). It would suffice, then, to sew about 3.5 kilograms of carbonized cork into the lining of a life-jacket to keep this man afloat and save him from drowning.' A remarkable step forward when one compares it to some of the absurd and fantastic devices invented around the same time.

The next milestone in the further development of life-saving gear was the inflatable life-jacket, inflated either automatically or by mouth. It began with the invention of suitable valves. In 1977 Otto and Max Mechnig of Berlin designed a valve in which the mouth-piece is depressed to admit air and released to close the valve (Fig. 206). With the type of valve common until then part of the air inevitably escaped as the screw top was replaced.

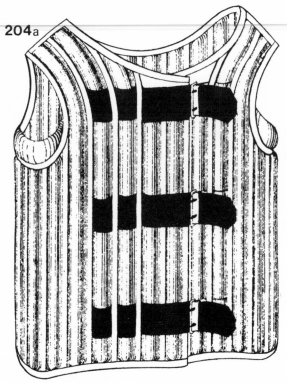

204a

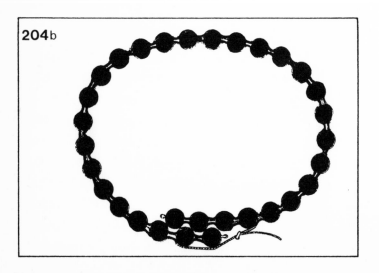

204b

In 1887 the Englishman Robert Dawson Kay designed an even better valve, in which the air tube was closed by a spring mechanism, which was released for inflating by simple lip pressure (Fig. 207). He had intended this mainly for use with a buoyancy collar, which we meet here for the first time in inflatable form.

The first inflatable life-belt was also a British invention. It was a straightforward lace-up belt that could be worn underneath or on top of clothing. It was made of watertight material and inflated by means of a valve (Fig. 208). Its inventor, William Hargreaves, does not mention in his patent specification of 1893 how, in an emergency, a person swimming in the water can get his mouth near the valve, but he does stress that 'at the front the belt has two larger pockets with considerably greater capacity, so that there is a concentration of buoyancy at the front of the body. This turns the body in such a way that the wearer can float on his back.' Here speaks a practical man who knows from experience which position a motionless person takes up in the water.

Practically-minded inventors also realized that the man overboard does not usually have much spare breath with which to inflate his buoyancy aid. They were, therefore, looking for new ways to make it self-inflating. The first attempts were still slightly fantastic:

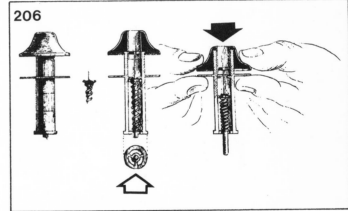

206

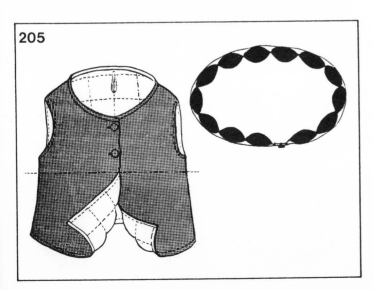

205

In 1899 the Frenchman H. Collin had a device patented in which water reacts with calcium carbide contained in the pockets of a life-jacket to make acetylene gas, which inflates the air chambers sewn into the front of the jacket (Fig. 209). The carbide cartridge is inserted into the pocket through a small hole at the bottom sealed by a screw-in plug. The cartridge is enveloped by some wide-meshed cloth, the pores of which are filled with bread dough. The bread dough is to prevent premature reaction of the carbide with the moisture in the air, but at the same time provides a wrapping which is easily dissolved by water entering the pocket.

If the wearer falls overboard, water enters the air chamber through a pin-hole in the valve and sets off the formation of gas. The gas pressure inside the

idea inspired Hans Kuhlmann of Buxweiler in Germany, who in 1900 developed an 'inflatable lining for buoyancy garments', which already resembled the air pockets in our modern life-jackets: 'Until now life-saving devices have suffered from the great disadvantage of being too clumsy or disfiguring to be worn permanently. These inflatable air-bags can be fitted into any piece of clothing without changing its appearance or being at all in the way.'

A characteristic feature are the vertical channels, which serve as stiffening and ensure that the appliance inflates evenly and does not lose its shape.

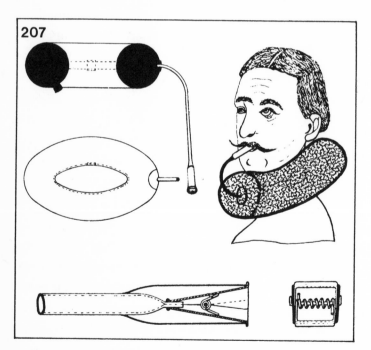

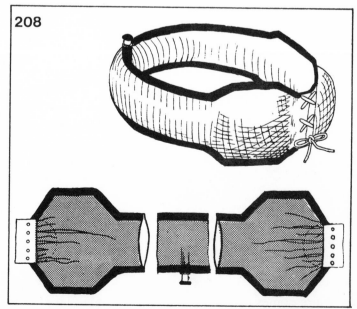

chamber then closes the valve, thus preventing the exit of gas as well as the entry of more water.

Whether this complicated process did, in fact, function as planned cannot be established. But undoubtedly the

Fig. 209   Inflatable pockets fitted into a suit by H. Collin, France, 1899.

In 1904 the Frenchman Emmanuel Manco-Schnurer designed a pressure valve on a cartridge filled with liquid or compressed gas (e.g. liquid carbon-dioxide), which is released into an inflatable container when pressure comes on the valve (See Figs 211a and 211b).

The principle is still in use today, but a valve which opens by twist action is now more commonly used than a pressure valve.

When Karl Bieber of Düsseldorf in Germany had his 'hollow walking stick with inflatable buoyancy bags inside' patented in 1902 (Figs 212a and 212b), he did not, alas, incorporate a gas cartridge in it. With its *two* buoyancy bags (as compared to one in previous models) it must have been the safest walking stick ever. It floats in a horizontal position, with the buoyancy bags (inflatable by mouth) at either end and still supports a man even if only one bag functions. These 'life-sticks' were kept handy on deck and are said to have been of great service to the crew on their doubtlessly hazardous way along the gang-plank when going ashore.

Anyone who had neither the means for a gas cartridge nor the breath to inflate his life-jacket by mouth could acquire, after August 1934, the inflating device developed by the Canadians George A. Evenden and George F. Wilson (Fig. 213), which 'enables a life-belt to be pumped up quickly and safely and in a manner easily understood and accomplished even by a non-swimmer' (Fig. 214).

It must be admitted that this fairly recent invention had very little to do with common sense. The device consists of a thing like a funnel, which is connected with the inflatable belt via a tube (Fig. 213). In an emergency this funnel is taken out of its case and held

Fig. 210 'Inflatable lining for buoyancy garments' by Hans Kuhlmann, Buxweiler, Germany, 1900.

Figs 211a and 211b Cartridge with pressure valve for inflating buoyancy aids by Emanuel Manco-Schnurer, France, 1904.

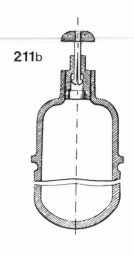

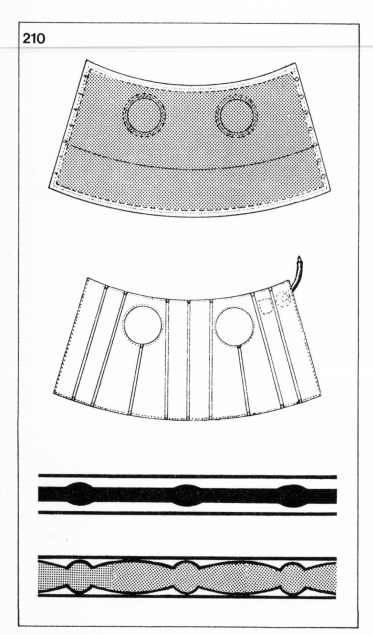

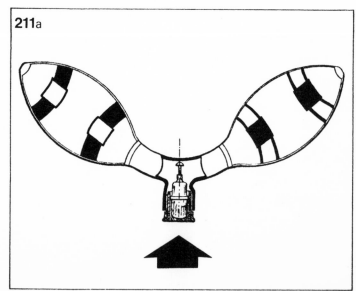

Figs 212a and 212b 'Walking stick with inflatable bags' by Karl Bieber, Düsseldorf, Germany, 1902.

Fig. 213 'Device for inflating a life-belt' by George A. Evenden and George F. Wilson, Canada, 1934.

212a

above the water with its opening facing downwards, so that it can fill with air. It is then pulled under water so that the (compressed!) air is pushed through the tube and inflates the belt—against the water pressure! This is repeated again and again . . . presumably until the person has drowned.

In 1906 the Krieger Shoe Company of Brooklyn, USA invented a rigid (or inflatable) 'life-belt which is open in front and is worn round the neck and shoulders'. It is specially shaped to fit the neck and shoulders (Fig. 215) and might be called the forerunner of the rigid 'Secumar' life-belt, which has proved itself in recent times.

In 1921 we come across another inflatable buoyancy collar (Fig. 216), which is open in front and can be closed by a snap fastening. It was invented by the American George Pallady and really ought to have initiated a development which did not, in fact, get under way until quite recently. This collar is divided into airtight sections so that it gives sufficient support to the head even when damaged. A collar of this type,

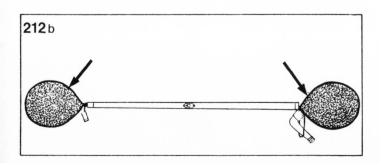

212b

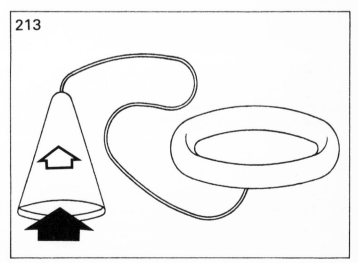

213

141

Fig. 214 This is the way the 'device for inflating a life-belt' by the Canadians George A. Evenden and George F. Wilson worked.

Fig. 215 Rigid shoulder-belt by the Krieger Shoe Company of Brooklyn, USA, 1906.

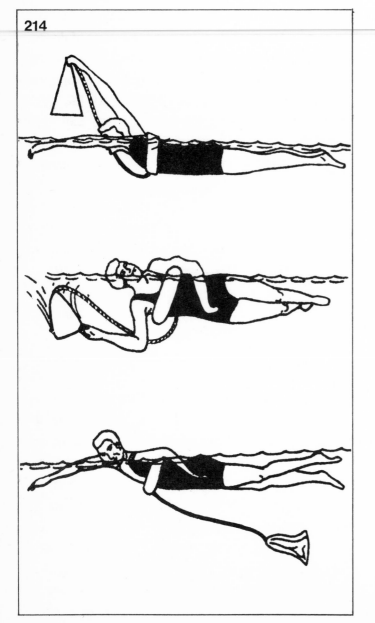

which supports the heaviest part of the body, i.e. the head, can be much smaller than a body-belt, which never completely rules out the danger of the head becoming submerged. While a 'man with head' has been calculated to need 3.5 kilograms (7.7 lbs) of buoyancy, a 'man without head' needs only about 2 kilograms (4.4 lbs).

Charles Frederic Sultemeyer of Chicago, USA, had designed a 'folding lifeboat with flexible floor and inflatable sides joined to the floor' as early as 1900, and this already had all the features of our modern inflatable boat (Fig. 217), but the manufacturers of

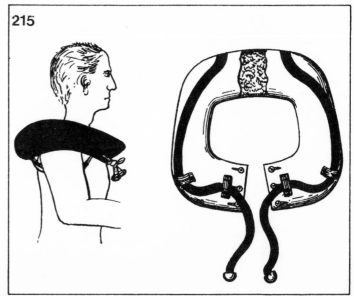

Fig.216   Buoyancy collar by George Pallady, USA, 1921.

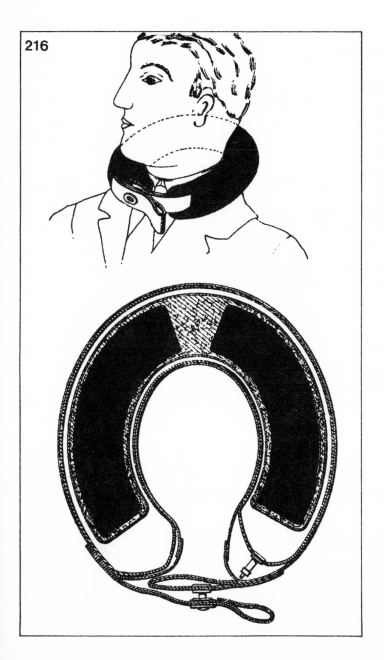

life-saving gear took no notice of this type of craft for many decades. On the other hand, all sorts of doubtful apparatus were patented, of which only very few could have been of practical use, among them a rope-work passenger gondola suspended from a cork life-ring as illustrated in Fig. 218. No matter which way up the ring fell into the water, the gondola would always hang downwards and afford ample room for a number of shipwrecked persons. They would, of course, get their feet rather wet. This life-raft was patented by the Charley Life Float Company of Boston, USA in 1902.

Rather more comfortable was the life-raft invented by Gustav Frank of Mannheim, Germany in 1923. It consisted of an inflatable ring with attached floor made of a folding, umbrella-type frame and an outer skin of watertight material (Fig. 219).

One of the forerunners of the proven one-man life-raft was the inflatable sack patented in 1923 by Gus Jordahn of Palm Beach, USA. This watertight sack was inflated through two sleeves, which were then knotted together to make a tight seal without the need of a valve (Figs 220a, 220b and 220c). This may have inspired the firm of Zodiac in their epoch-making design: the inflatable boat with a wooden transom. The purpose of this was not only to provide a firm anchorage point for an outboard motor but also to make the boat more rigid. In previous designs (cf Charles Sultemeyer's, Fig. 217) the inflatable tube had gone continuously all the way round the boat.

Fig. 217 'Folding lifeboat with flexible floor and inflatable sides' by Charles Frederic Sultemeyer, Chicago,
USA, 1900.

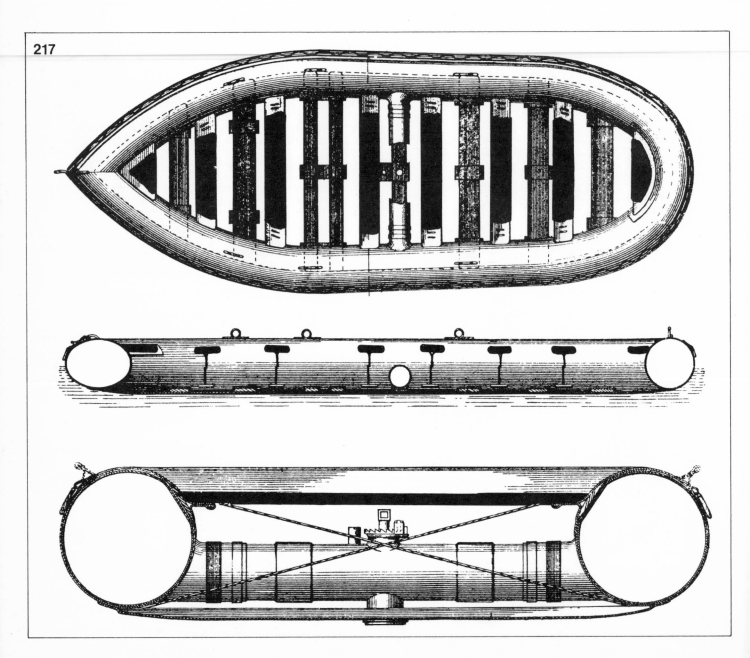

217

Fig. 218 Inflatable life-raft with net gondola by the Charley Life Float Company, Boston, USA, 1902.

Fig. 219 Circular life-raft with inflatable sides by Gustav Frank, Mannheim, Germany, 1923.

Figs 220a, 220b and 220c Inflatable sack by Gus Jordahn, Palm Beach, USA, 1923.

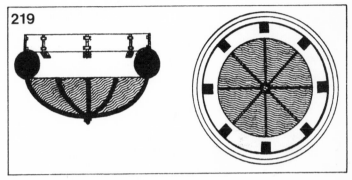

219

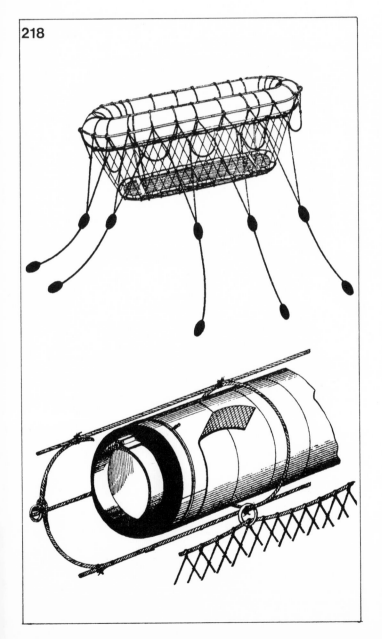

218

In conclusion let us take a look at some patents which aimed at making lifebuoys more easily visible in the water and facilitating the search for persons overboard. As early as 1881 the Englishman Robert Whitby designed the lifebuoy illustrated in Fig. 221, which consisted of a ring with airtight partitions, two chains of different length for hanging on to and a tube on

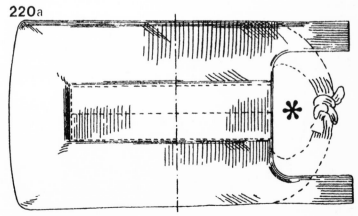

220a

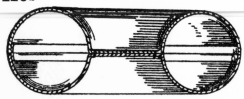

220b

There are also records of early attempts to solve the problem of how to light up a lifebuoy. Some of them strike us as rather fantastic, like the night-light by Wilhelm Küpper of Wangerooge in Germany, which

either side, weighted at the base, to which flares and markers were attached.

Willi Hinz of Hamburg, Germany, improved on this patent in 1907 by marking the ring with a short flag mast with a heavy plate at the base (Fig. 222). As the flag adjusts itself parallel to the wind direction, the plate sets at right angles to wind and leeway and resists the tendency of the lifebuoy to drift away with the wind.

221

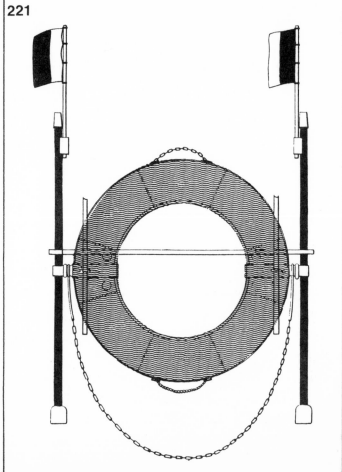

220c

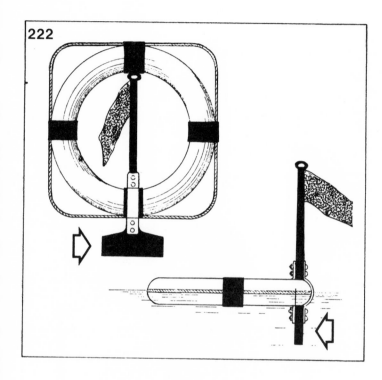

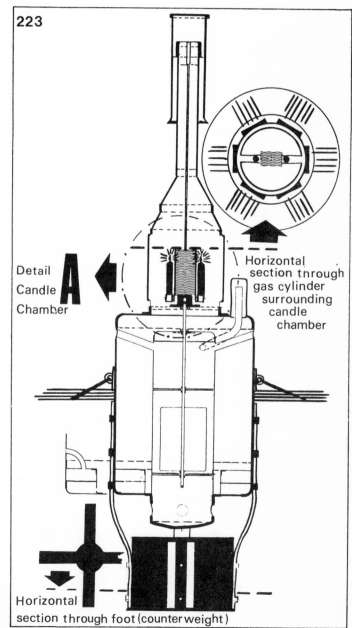

Detail Candle Chamber

Horizontal section through gas cylinder surrounding candle chamber

Horizontal section through foot (counterweight)

was patented in 1888 (Figs 223 and 224). It works on candles, which are automatically lit by matches when the lifebuoy moves in a seaway. As it is dropped into the water, it has to be completely submerged so that one of its compartments can fill with water. As a result a float is raised, which pushes matches through an opening and in doing so strikes them against a rough surface. The float not only causes the candles to be lit but also opens a valve, which otherwise keeps the chimney shut, so that the combustion fumes can escape. Obviously *dead* reliable!

Fig. 224 Detail of candle chamber in the lifebuoy-light by Wilhelm Kupper, Wangerooge, 1888.

Fig. 225 Gas-light lifebuoy with automatic ignition by Conrad Wiese and Max Groschner, Hamburg, Germany, 1899.

Perhaps Conrad Wiese and Max Gröschner of Hamburg in Germany were more successful in 1899 with their lifebuoy illuminated by an acetylene gas light with automatic ignition (Fig. 225). The gas is formed

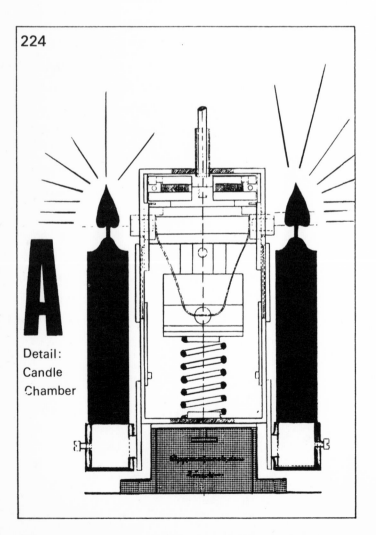

224

Detail:
Candle
Chamber

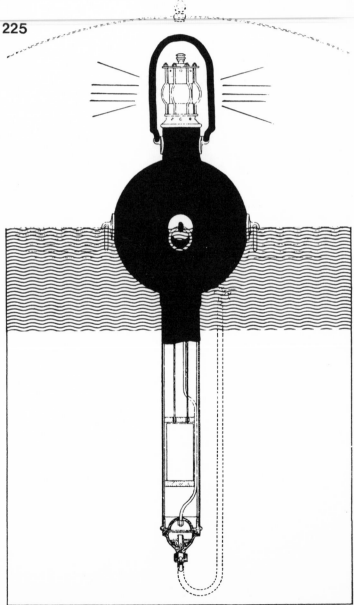

225

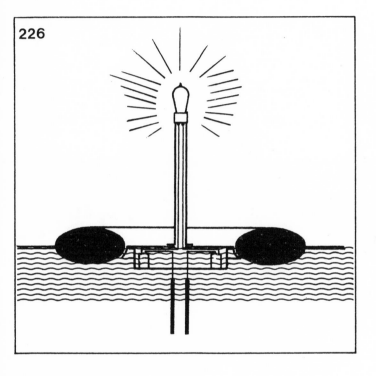

226

as water enters, and a rubber ball, which is inflated by the gas pressure, closes an electric circuit. A platinum strip begins to glow and in turn ignites the gas in the burner. Finally the flame melts a lead wire to interrupt the electric circuit.

Not long afterwards, in 1903, the first electrically illuminated lifebuoy was patented by Rudolf E. Hellmund in New York. While in previous types of lifebuoy the electric circuit was closed by a float or by springs that were released as the buoy made contact with the water, in this case the water itself acts as conductor to close the circuit (Fig. 226).

We may smile superciliously at some of these ideas, which strike us as ludicrous and even crack-brained. But we must not forget that most of them were conceived years or even decades before the tragedy of the *Titanic*. Then, as later, even sensible and useful patents were never put to any use and eventually fell into oblivion. But old patents can give rise to new developments, and some of them have been revived in recent times.

This early hydrofoil craft was built in 1911 by S. E. Saunders Ltd of Cowes, Isle of Wight, England, for the Frenchman Monsieur Ravaud. It was 19 ft long and fitted with a 50 hp motor driving an air propeller.